A NEW
REFORMATION

A New REFORMATION

Creation Spirituality
and the
Transformation of Christianity

MATTHEW FOX

Inner Traditions
Rochester, Vermont

Inner Traditions
One Park Street
Rochester, Vermont 05767
www.InnerTraditions.com

LIBRARY OF CONGRESS CATALOGING-IN-PUBLICATION DATA

Fox, Matthew, 1940–
    A new reformation : creation spirituality and the transformation of Christianity / Matthew Fox.
        p. cm.
    Includes bibliographical references.
    ISBN 1-59477-123-5 (pbk.)
    1. Spirituality. 2. Christianity—Controversial literature.
I. Title.
    BL624.F683 2006
    230— dc22

                                                    2005032559

Printed and bound in Canada by Transcontinental Printing

10 9 8 7 6 5 4 3 2 1

Text design and layout by Virginia Scott Bowman
This book was typeset in Goudy and Agenda with Abbess and Skreech Caps as the display typefaces

This book is dedicated to my 107 (at last count) sister and brother theologians silenced and threatened under Pope John Paul II and Pope Benedict XVI (formerly Cardinal Ratzinger):

. . . with sadness at the lost service to the church in translating tradition to contemporary culture;

. . . with compassion for those theologians who have had abuse heaped upon them and who have been expelled from work and communities and their vocation;

. . . with holy outrage that a pope who shouted so loudly his opposition to abortion chose for twenty-five years to abort the life of thought, dialogue, new ideas, and creative movements in the church, all of which it is the special vocation of theologians to midwife;

. . . in solidarity with those who are without a voice due to political, economic, social, gender, or gender preference oppression;

. . . and with deep trust that the Spirit, who always prefers *biophilia* (love of life) to *necrophilia* (love of death), and is so much vaster, more fecund, and more imaginative than any man-made forms of religion or empire, might invigorate religion with new forms and awaken spirituality, thus giving hope, promise, and adventure to the newest generations.

Contents

Acknowledgments

I am deeply grateful to all those who have helped with this book, including Jim Garrison for his encouragement; Jorg Wichmann and Peter Shipton for their translation into German; Larry Marshall for his research on fundamentalists in their own words; and Dennis Edwards, Debra Martin, and Javier Garcia Lemus for their support. Thanks to Father Bernard Lynch for use of his letter on pages 50–53, Ned Leavitt for his support as my book agent, Elaine Cissi for her conscientious copyediting, Rev. Jim Roberts and others for responding to the call for a New Reformation, and Anne Weifenbach for her leadership in Wittenberg.

Journey to Wittenberg, Creation Spirituality, and the Transformation of Christianity

This book was born in a very short period of time after thirty-five years of intellectual and spiritual work. Allow me to explain.

At the time that Cardinal Ratzinger was elected pope, I was preparing to go to Frankfurt, Germany, to fulfill a speaking invitation I had accepted a year earlier. The occasion was Pentecost Sunday and the invitation was to give a public lecture and a day's workshop at the Bad Herrenalb Healing Center in Frankfurt. Pentecost Sunday is the traditional feast day celebrating the birth of the Church—that is, the occasion written of in the Acts of the Apostles when the disciples of Jesus, scared and huddled together after Jesus' death and departure, were suddenly struck by "tongues of fire," which enabled them to preach and speak of their experience of Jesus and the Christ in Jesus. The powerful passage from the prophet Joel that is identified with this feast promises that "your old folks shall dream dreams, and your young ones see visions" (Acts 2.16–21). In Europe, unlike America, Pentecost is a significant feast day that often includes a holiday from work.

With this assignment staring me in the face, with Cardinal Ratzinger's unusual election to the papacy having just occurred, and with much e-mail pouring in to me saying such things as "I am leaving the Ratzinger Church" and "This is the end of the line for Roman Catholicism, even though I have hung in there all these difficult years," I was aware that it would not be business as usual—or lecturing as usual—when I arrived in Germany. Given these circumstances, I could not in conscience speak on the Pentecost theme of rebirth of the church. How could I steer in positive directions people's moral outrage? What of the fact that Ratzinger was the first German-born pope in six hundred years and my lecture was to address Germans? How candid ought I to be with my German audience?

What to do?

I prayed about it and one night, at 3:30 in the morning, I was awakened with an idea: Why not draw up some theses, just as Martin Luther had done five hundred years ago, that would speak to my concerns and those of the people from whom I was hearing? Why not reenact Luther's protest: the nailing of his theses to the church door in Wittenberg?

I sat down and began to draft some theses of my own. I thought there might be fifteen or twenty lurking inside of me, but by the time the sun rose around 5:30 a.m., I found that I had poured out ninety-five theses. One after another they had tumbled out of me, and I was amazed. When I read them over a few days later, I did not change them at all, beyond rearranging three or four. What you read in this book are those ninety-five theses written during that night and early morning. They do, I believe, represent a certain reformation—and indeed transformation—of church and religion for our times.

On to Wittenberg

I then traveled to Germany with Dr. Jim Garrison, the new president of the University of Creation Spirituality (now known as Wisdom University), and once there, we met with Peter Shipton, a graduate of Wisdom University living in Germany, who, along with Jorg Wichman, was kind enough to assist in helping to translate the theses into German. Following my initial presentation, I met Anne Weifenbach, a German woman who knew English well and who accompanied us to Wittenberg, providing inestimable logistical support and womanly advice along the way.

Attending my presentation at Bad Herrenalb was the editor of Publik Forum, a very respected ecumenical theological journal in Germany. After I finished, we met for two hours, during which he explored in more detail my efforts and my intention to go to Wittenberg with my new theses. At the same time, I learned more of his story, including how Meister Eckhart, the great Dominican mystic and prophet of the fourteenth century, was responsible for his conversion from an ex-Christian to a Christian once again. True to his word, he published the ninety-five theses in his journal and created a German blog (www.publikforum.de) on which many people have been discussing the theses and ideas presented in this book. In this forum two principle questions have been posed: 1) Do we need a New Reformation today? and 2) Which of the ninety-five theses are the most important? (A blog for English speakers to discuss the New Reformation can be found at www.matthewfox.org.)

During our trip to Wittenberg, several eye-opening events occurred. Before we arrived we learned that permission was required to perform an action at the church door, so Peter and Anne headed to the city hall for the permission slip as soon as we reached our destination. At first, the city officials told us, "You have only one hour and you must be at least forty-five feet from the historic door on which Luther pounded his theses." When asked why, they responded, "Because we do not want you interfering with tourists who come to see the doors." This was quite telling; in fact, I have written in this book about how much of Christianity (especially European Christianity) has become museum-like and, in this case, the stuff of tourists' photo opportunities. It was as if an effort to make Christianity alive again in the twenty-first century would have to take a back seat to kowtowing to camera-toting tourists—note that the officials did not mention *pilgrims*. Sure enough, during the hours we were at the church door, a number of tourists on buses and individuals with cameras arrived, snapped pictures, and left—often within a two-minute period. Lots of tourists, very few pilgrims. As it turned out, after much haggling, Anne and Peter talked the town officials into allowing us to perform our action right at the church doors rather than forty-five feet away.

During our action, a large tourist bus drove up and a number of English-speaking black people disembarked and approached the historic doors. I asked one of them, "Where are you from?" imagining they might be from Chicago. "South Africa," he responded as their tour guide spoke to them about the doors and their meaning. When she finished, after about ten minutes, I spoke up: "Excuse me," I said, "I am a theologian visiting from the United States and I am here not just to look back five hundred years in history, but to make some history today. We feel Christianity needs a New Reformation. If you stay, you can hear how we might bring this about."

Surprisingly, the tour guide got very huffy and snorted: "We are on a tight schedule—how dare you interfere with our trip! Everyone is to get back on the bus immediately." With that she marched off, tourists in check behind her. A number of the travelers, however, held back and came up to me and said: "We would love to stay behind and learn more, but we are foreigners and we have to get on the bus or be lost here!"

Nailing the theses to the church doors proved to require more than merely convincing officials to grant us access. Because the doors are no longer wooden but metal (now engraved with Luther's words), we had to fashion a wooden frame to which we could then fasten the ninety-five new theses. Interestingly, I found that the pounding of the nails served as a genuinely archetypal act: The sound of the nails entering the wooden frame was not unlike the sound of nails being driven into a cross. After we posted the theses, I explained to those gathered the significance of the theses and why we needed a rebirth of the church, and then opened the ceremony to questions. Someone asked, "Is this call for a New Reformation an issue for the Roman Catholic Church alone, brought about particularly by the election of Cardinal Ratzinger?"

What a very important question! Just the day before, we had been in Erfurt, Germany, the city where Luther was ordained a priest and where Meister Eckhart served as prior for four years. There we asked a Lutheran pastor who showed us around the Predikekirche, the church of Eckhart's day, what he thought of our plans to go to Wittenberg to call for a New Reformation. He replied: "Today, only 5 to 8 percent of Lutherans in Germany practice their faith. Of course we need a New Reformation."

This book is not addressed solely to the Roman Catholic Church (which is currently mired in the deep corruption of its hierarchy, evidenced by the hypocrisy and horror of the cover-up of the priestly pedophilia and other scandals, including the canonization of a fascist admirer of Hitler). The call to Reformation is a call to Protestant churches as well. While the Protestant tradition does not suffer from the same public display of corruption experienced by the Roman Catholic Church right now, nevertheless it has very much lost its juice as a protesting and prophetic body. It has fallen into comfort and, in the worst cases, such as the instance of fundamentalism in America, into sleeping with the imperial powers, which lends such powers religious legitimization.

Present-day Protestantism suffers from apathy, or what our ancestors called *acedia*, a lack of energy or a kind of spiritual sloth. Descriptors I would apply to today's Protestantism are: anemic, tired, boring, incurious, unadventurous, emasculated, compromising, confused, depressed (a recent study found that about 80 percent of the pastors in one liberal branch of Protestantism are taking antidepressant drugs!), unmystical, lost, irrelevant, preoccupied with trivia, uninspired, one-dimensional, and burned out. All the issues that these adjectives imply are in fact spiritual in nature. Protestantism often lacks a profound spirituality (the word *spirituality* was rarely in its theological vocabulary until very recently) and this lack is beginning to show. What has happened to the protest in Protestantism? What will it take to bring it back? Protestantism has a proud and profound intellectual heritage, yet it is allowing itself to be mowed over by anti-intellectual fundamentalism, which has hijacked Jesus, Christ, and Christianity as a whole.

Yes, at this time in history Protestantism, like Catholicism, needs a radical overhaul—a New Reformation and new transformation. Both need to move from religion to spirituality.

The Origin of the Ninety-five Theses

One person who has read the theses told me: "The ninety-five theses are actually a summary of your previous twenty-five books." This is true; while they poured out of me in the late-night and early-morning hours, they have been in me for many years, not so much as theses but as lessons I had learned while trying to bring to life a critical spirituality in our troubled times.

While I pursued my doctoral studies in Paris in the late 1960s, it was my good fortune to study with such amazing historians of spirituality as Pere Chenu and Abbé Louis Cognet. These people set me intellectually on my way, and my journey has carried me into many regions of culture and spiritual interaction, including work with scientists, activists, feminists, artists, and biblical scholars.

It has also led me to reinvent forms of teaching so that we may educate more than just the head in our learning institutions. For thirty years I have been practicing these forms of education, first at the Institute in Culture and Creation Spirituality, and then at the University of Creation Spirituality. My path has also led me to work with young people to create postmodern forms of worship such as our Cosmic Masses, begun nine years ago and sponsored by the Friends of Creation Spirituality. These Masses integrate dance, images, rap, and electronic music with the liturgy.

Yes, when I read these theses, I do indeed recognize statements about issues I have wrestled with or conclusions

I have come to through my writings and teaching and lec-turing over the years. In many ways these ninety-five theses are a summary of my understanding of the creation spiritu-ality tradition and what it offers us today.

1

The Reformation Yesterday and Today

Approximately five hundred years ago, a religious renewal was launched on German soil in the town of Wittenberg by an Augustinian monk and theologian named Martin Luther. This Reformation, as it came to be called, was a revolution heard around the European world. Its result was a split between the Roman Catholic version of Christianity and what we have come to know as Protestant Christianity. Like any great historical event, the Reformation was the product of many combined forces. Among the most significant were the following:

1. **The invention of the printing press.** This technological achievement effectively democratized knowledge and the power that results from knowledge and information. The Reformation was the religious response to the invention of the printing press—after all, the first book printed was

the Bible, which was disseminated in the vernacular and became available to national groups and individuals as never before. The printing press effectively launched the modern era of scholarship and textual analysis that we know as the Enlightenment. The development of modern science and widespread education followed.

2. **The rise of the nation-state.** European nation-states eagerly accepted Martin Luther's break with the Holy Roman Empire and the Roman Church, which had legitimized that empire and held it together. The subsequent rise of nationalism motivated the rapid invasion of conquered lands and peoples by European nation-states and the accumulation of riches taken from the indigenous peoples of the Americas, Africa, Pacific Islands, and Asia. Booty in the form of slaves, as well as gold, silver, and other riches, were carted off to Europe.

3. **The corruption of the Roman Catholic Church in the highest places.** Leading up to the time of the Reformation, defective theology, the selling of indulgences, simony, nepotism, and greed ruled the popes and their fiefdoms. The faithful, who were taxed to increase the wealth of the Roman Church but who shared nothing of the money and privileges that accrued, began to feel great anger and resentment. It was difficult to see any resemblance between a corrupt papacy and Jesus the founder of Christianity. Apocalyptic slogans characterizing Rome as the "anti-Christ" and "whore of Babylon" captured the popular imagination.

4. **The rise of an educated elite.** Martin Luther owed much to the humanist scholarship of his day and was among those who could read and translate Biblical languages. In fact, he translated the entire Bible into German. This made for an intellectual empowerment that could not be satisfied by mere repetition of dogmatic shibboleths that doctrinaire churchmen repeated ad nauseam.

Today, in 2005, we find ourselves in a situation analogous to that experienced by Luther in his time, but with added dimensions of seriousness. Human beings, along with thousands of other species on the planet, face a peril of potential extinction that has not been witnessed on the earth in 65 million years. The last time such a spasm occurred was when the dinosaurs disappeared. Ironically, human knowledge and technology are the most significant causes of this potential extinction. Isn't this another sign that religion is not accomplishing its task, that religion is powerful in the wrong ways and powerless to effect change in the right ways? The population explosion in the human race, the growing canyon between the haves and have-nots, rich and poor, powerful and powerless, cry out for attention. So too do the rights of minorities—women, people of color, tribal and indigenous people, and gay and lesbian people.

Among today's forces that parallel those at the time of the Reformation are:

1. **The electronic revolution that began in the 1960s.** Analogous to the wave of information that spread after the launch of the printing press, this revolution launched what we now call the postmodern era in which the computer chip, Internet, e-mail, portable phones, and instant global communication have profound political and religious implications. With the electronic revolution, a postmodern civilization was born.

2. **The waning of nation-states and the rise of multinational, global corporations.** Such "multinationals" are the sole rival of the United Nations, which they effectively skewer, ignore, and malign. (Witness President Bush's appointed U.S. representative to the United Nations, John Bolton, who spoke of cutting ten stories from the headquarters of the United Nations itself.) Globalization is introducing new forces and relationships among nations and economies. The end of the Cold War and the collapse of the Soviet empire left only one empire standing—the United States, whose growth in power exacerbates worldwide the hatred and resentment directed toward it, as expressed by, for example, the events on 9/11.

   The sharp contrast between rich nations (having one third of the world's population) and poor nations (having two thirds of the world's population) also characterizes the state of affairs today. Studies show that we would need four planets to sustain human life if everyone practiced the lifestyles of North Americans and Europeans.

Clearly the American and European lifestyles are not sustainable as they are.

3. **The corruption and ineffectiveness of Western Religion.** This is becoming increasingly apparent for all to see. The Protestant era has long since ceased to exist and Protestantism finds itself in an extremely tired state: Its churches are effectively empty in most northern European countries and America, and little energy remains in organizations except that aroused when people are invited to express their opposition to gays and gay clergy.

One aspect of the corruption of religion in the West is the political involvement of rabid fundamentalists and the role of those evangelical leaders who preach a contemporary apocalypse. These individuals actually seem to want a nuclear war to occur—preferably in Israel so that Jesus can return on a cloud and take his chosen ones to heaven. In America, these people are determined to obscure the long-held law of separation of church and state, and politicians willing to sell their souls to get elected are busy obliging.

Meanwhile, in spite of television's fawning over the made-for-television theater of the papacy and its unending effort to build a cult of personality around the figure of the pope in order to increase its viewing audience, Roman Catholicism has hit a new low in it spotty history—one matched only by the corrupt papacies of the Borgias in Martin Luther's time. One proof of this is the coddling of pedophile clergy by those of the Roman Church hierarchy, such as Cardinal Law (who has since been given a plum assignment: overseeing a fourth-century Basilica in Rome). While Law was defending pedophile priests, Cardinal Ratzinger (now Pope Benedict XVI) was expelling prophetic priests and theologians who led liberation movements of the poor and the oppressed (including women, peasants, defenders of the rain forest, and those seeking democracy in Central and South America).

By persecuting theologians and shutting down theological inquiry and institutions of learning, the highest prelates of the Roman Church have deliberately and purposely replaced theology with ideology and created a generation of cardinals and bishops who take oaths of loyalty and who march lockstep to orders from the top without passing them through their own consciences. It is loyalty, not intellectual acumen or moral courage, that has recommended them to the positions of authority they now hold. Pedophilia and clerical abuse, hierarchal complicity in such abuse, the inadequate role of women in the Roman Church, gay and lesbian rights: Such prelates are not allowed to address these issues. Instead of leaders, we are given sycophants. Any papacy that canonizes a man who praised Hitler—namely Father Josemaría Escrivá, the fascist priest and founder of Opus Dei, a so-called religious order whose slogan might be "A preferential option for the rich and powerful"—must be skewed.

It is time to tell the truth. "Even the rocks shall shout out" declared the historical Jesus. So too, at this low period in Catholic and church history, it is time to let our moral outrage speak. The church has been hijacked by those committed to a preferential option for the rich and the powerful. Do we determine to take it back, or simply move on?

4. **An Awakened Scholarship.** Just as five hundred years ago new scholarship was unleashed to buttress a deeper understanding of scripture and early Church history, so today significant scholarship—including archeological findings, the rediscovery of ancient texts, progress in the two-hundred-year-old quest for the "historical Jesus," and the development of women's theology and history—has gifted us with new and substantive information about the words, the people, and the teachings of Jesus, Paul, and individuals in the early Christian community. Mixing these findings with our awareness of the origins of Christianity is part of this study.

Likewise contributing to an awakened intellectual life are the discoveries about the history, size, and unfolding of our universe; the consequent birthing of a new creation story, with all the wonder it arouses; the insights and methodologies derived from the psychological and sociological sciences; the rise of mystical science; the discovery of chaos theory; and so much more.

What is the good news in all this? It is that we can start anew, that a New Reformation for a new millennium is upon us. The current papacy can run the Vatican Museum and St. Peter's Basilica, but we can let go of religion and begin to get serious about spiritual practice. Protestantism can shed its apathy and ask not "What did Luther or Calvin say five hundred years ago?" but rather "What would Luther and Calvin say and do in today's global ecological and ecclesial crisis? We can draw on, rather than neglect, the riches of the Roman Church's mystics and prophets of past and present and work on interfaith activism and spiritual practice with those of other faith traditions.

It is time get on with many tasks that await us today. At stake is the sustainability of our species and the planet as we know it. Issues such as resisting the spread of empire, advocacy of the use of condoms in a time of AIDS, birth control advocacy in a time of population explosion, equitable distribution of the world's goods, the use of clean and renewable energy, the importance of community life, the elimination of poverty, the creation of good work, the defense of minorities including gays and lesbians—all these call to us. Deep ecumenism and interfaith movements allow Christians and others to renew their spiritual roots. But the primary obstacle to reaching an interfaith identity, as the Dalai Lama has observed, is "a bad relationship with one's own faith tradition." Those espousing the theology of the Punitive Father who seeks obedience at all costs harbor a bad relationship with their own faith tradition. They know

Original Sin but not Original Blessing. They cannot participate in the interfaith movement. And very often, as in the case of Pope Benedict XVI, who has criticized Buddhism, Hinduism, Protestantism, Native traditions, and goddess religions, they do not want to participate. Yet the Divine Wisdom and Original Blessing tradition has always been about an interfaith perspective.

What, then, is the good news in all this? That we can start anew. That a New Reformation for a new millennium is upon us.

2

Two Christianities:
Time for a Divorce?

For the New Reformation to take place the West must acknowledge what is now obvious for all to see: There are two Christianities in our midst. One worships a Punitive Father and teaches the doctrine of Original Sin. It is patriarchal in nature, links readily to fascist powers of control, and demonizes women, the earth, other species, science, and gays and lesbians. It builds on fear and supports empire building.

The other Christianity recognizes the Original Blessing from which all being derives. It recognizes awe, rather than sin and guilt, as the starting point of true religion. It thus marvels at today's scientific findings about the wonders of the fourteen-billion-year journey of the universe that has brought our being into existence and the wonders of our special home, the earth. It prefers trust over fear and an understanding of a divinity who is source of all things, as much mother as father, as much female as male. It is an emerging "woman church" that does not exclude men, and tries to consider the whole earth as a holy temple. Because it honors creation, it does not denigrate what creation has accomplished, which includes the 8 percent of the human population that is gay or lesbian and those 464+ other species with gay and lesbian populations. It considers evil to be a choice that we make as humans—one that separates us from our common good—and that we can unmake.

For some time, Christian churches, both Protestant and Catholic, have been trying to coexist within these two traditions. But with world developments being what they are—with the buttressing of the American empire under George Bush by fundamentalist ideology and religious forces, with "faith-based communities" encroaching on the principle of separation of church and state, with the ignoring of issues of poverty and economic justice, it is time to separate these two versions of Christianity.

It is very difficult to imagine the historical Jesus, who took on the Roman Empire of his day, being at all pleased with the cheerleaders of the American empire rallying in his name. St. Paul also took on the Roman Empire—indeed the phrase he applied to Jesus, "son of God," was borrowed not so much from Jewish theology as from the Empire's theology, which taught that Augustus was the son of God.

In fact, as a rabbi taught me, "everyone who is living out God's wisdom deserves to be called a son or daughter of God." We can hope that this includes all of us, along with Jesus, who lived so generously a life of wisdom.

The recent *coup d'eglise* (takeover of the Church) by Pope Benedcit XVI is one more wake up call that it is time to put an end to the Christian flirtation with empire building that occupies not only American politics but the politics of organizations such as the Catholic group Opus Dei. This organization, supported by Pope John Paul II and the current pope, searches for power in the financial and media capitals of the world. Due to the organization's secretive nature, its true intentions are kept under wraps. Because Opus Dei represents a preferential option for the rich and powerful, it is very difficult to see its connection to the teachings and person of Jesus.

It is time, then, that the two Christianities part ways. Pope Benedict and his 112 cardinals, whom he helped to appoint and who elected him pope, and all the bishops of the Roman Catholic Church, whom he also appointed (contrary to centuries of tradition dictating that bishops are chosen more or less locally) should be left to deal with their crisis of priestly pedophilia and the financial demands ensuing from their mismanagement of the Church.

The rest of the world must be allowed to get on with living life in depth—with biophilia (love of life), rather than necrophilia (love of death). Let us "let the dead bury the dead," as Jesus taught, and move ahead with a spirituality for the twenty-first century. Let the museum church be unto itself and let spirituality replace religion. Let Catholics no longer hide in the pews, hoping not to be seen. Let them find a conscience and stand up and act.

With spirituality as the basis of a New Reformation, a new renaissance—indeed, a rebirth of humanity—is once again possible, with a vision that is earth-honoring and oriented toward ecologic, economic, gender, social, and political justice. A New Reformation will seek mightily to balance female with male elements and to honor in every way the Mother-Father God of divine wisdom. It will consider the morality of keeping the earth beautiful and healthy to be at least as important as the morality of keeping human relationships beautiful and healthy.

This new humanity will have a vision of compassion that will render sustainable our lives and our planet, for what is just is sustainable. What is unjust, however, is unsustainable; it falls apart and leads to war, resentment, and violence. A new spiritual vision will focus not on religion, but spirituality, and in doing so will no longer serve empires and their aspirations, for empires legitimize their violence in the name of religion. A New Reformation will acknowledge the wisdom that emanates from all the world's spiritual traditions, with an authentically humble understanding that no one culture and no one way is the path to the Source. Interfaith movements and deep ecumenism will be necessary ingredients of a spirituality for the twenty-first century.

The split between the two existing versions of Christianity is not disappearing; on the contrary, it is widening. The issue of homosexuality is splitting the Anglican, Roman Catholic, Lutheran, Presbyterian, and Methodist churches. Some churches such as the United Church of Christ, Unity Church, United Church of Canada, Quakers, and Unitarian Universalism have left this issue behind them. They are already part of the divine wisdom tradition and deserve to be joined by those of us from the more "catholic" traditions, which spend far too much energy and time on trying to reform or conform to structures that are old, obsolete, and museum-like. This has led to the committing of numerous sins of omission, which are always sins against justice.

In turning our backs on these traditions, we leave them not because we dislike the people within them. On the contrary, at this dangerous time we leave them in order to live more fully the future to which they once called us. We leave them in order to carry on their best values, which are being tarnished by fear, tiredness, institutional rot, prejudice masquerading as tradition, and just plain necrophilia.

We leave the museum-like Christianity as we would a burning building—seizing what is most valuable and letting go of the rest. We take what is best from the old ways and leave behind what is unnecessarily burdensome, such as St. Augustine's teachings about sex, which lead to opposition to birth control and condom use even in an age of AIDS and to vilification of gays and lesbians.

The fundamentalist strains in all religions have a great deal in common with each other, regardless of the religions they represent. Fundamentalism from the Taliban (Islam), the Vatican (Catholic), and the Bible Belt (Protestant), as well as such movements in Judaism and Hinduism, share many mind-sets. In fact, it seems that Jerry Falwell and Pope Benedict XVI have more in common in their worldview and ideology than the pope does with theologian priests such as Leonardo Boff, Hans Kung, or myself, despite the fact that we four claim to be from the Catholic tradition. More than many Catholics themselves, Southern Baptists are in line with the ideology of Pope John Paul II and Pope Benedict XVI, which subjugates women and denounces gays, condoms, and abortion.

How is this possible? Fundamentalism has become a religion unto itself, whether it is translated through Osama bin Laden, Jerry Falwell, or Pope Benedict. It is a religion based on control, on dominant and domineering patriarchy, on the notion that it is in the right while everyone else is wrong, that those who follow it will be saved while everyone else is damned.

But what is the origin of this certainty?

I think it comes from several sources: a fear of chaos, a fear of the feminine, and a fear of trust. Above all, it comes from the wound inflicted by the Punitive Father. All fundamentalists have father wounds. Not just our personal experience but our very culture leaves us with father wounds. We are told, for example, that the universe, the home of Father Sky, is a junkyard of inert machine parts—the basic story emanating from Newton's view of the universe, which dominated for many generations in the modern era and which deeply wounds the masculine soul in particular.

This is so because men retreat into themselves; men must be able to project their greatness into the vast universe. When the cosmos is no longer considered vast, their greatness gets appropriated locally, through violence and war, hatred and power trips—and these characterize not only the fundamentalist impulse but also its political projection onto fascism in its many forms.

Interestingly, the ideology of Original Sin, first named by St. Augustine in the fourth century, when the Catholic Church was inheriting the Roman Empire, expresses perfectly the Punitive Father ideology: God punishes us just as he punished Adam and Eve. In fact, we are punished for their sin before we are even born. We come with a blot on our existence, in need of outside redemption. In the eyes of the Catholic Church, we are all guilty of something—of existence, of being born.

Of course, few parents believe in Original Sin. Indigenous peoples, Eastern Christians, Buddhists, and Jews do not believe in it either. Augustinian Christians, however, fiercely believe in it. To fundamentalists who espouse the notion of a Punitive Father, we must cower in everyday life and hate ourselves—thus our salvation lies in lining up and being good, obedient, docile citizens of the empire and the church that supports the empire.

The great mystic Meister Eckhart observed that "all the names we give to God come from an understanding of ourselves." This means that to believe in a Punitive Father is to believe in our own guilt and our own need for punishment, which we then project onto others. Guilt and punishment go hand in hand, making for "good" religion (based on the deep need for salvation), but the two are very dangerous sociologically and psychologically. In this context, religious sadism and masochism play an important role.

To teach people, especially young ones, that they are anything but images of God and heirs of divine creativity and responsibility is very dangerous. It leads to low esteem, low expectations, diminished compassion, increased fear, feelings of inferiority and inadequacy—the perfect setup for addictions not only to alcohol and drugs and shopping and sex, but to a religion of the Punitive Father and to its representatives. A counselor I know who has worked a great deal with alcoholics tells me that they often give up their chemical addiction when they "find God," but unfortunately the God they find is often a Punitive Father. The result of this is that they return to alcohol abuse.

The names and images we give to divinity are important. They matter deeply, saying volumes about who we believe we are and are not. For example, we may see God as "artist of artists" (Thomas Aquinas), the "great zither player of the universe" (Alan of Lille), "Source without a source" (Thomas Aquinas), "Life" (Hildegard of Bingen), "Music" (Hildegard of Bingen), or "Mother" (Julien of Norwich). But it is altogether different to see God as avenger, judge, punisher, maker of hell.

A Punitive Father religion and culture are pessimistic, control-oriented, uncreative, warlike, and sad and angry.

They banish from their religion the child-and-mother principle, which is the icon for compassion. Supplanting compassion are punishment and scolding. In fact, fundamentalism is full of punishment and scolding, shame and guilt. The late Pope John Paul II forever scolded theologians and women, liberation priests and bishops, artists, and of course gays and lesbians. Certainly, this made him very popular with those who felt the need to be scolded, with those who needed a Punitive Father on earth to serve as a vicar of the Punitive Father in heaven.

3

Fundamentalists
in Their Own Words

The Fundamentalist Christian mind-set has hijacked the name Jesus and the term Christ and the word Christianity. Yet many fundamentalist Christians have never studied the rich and diverse history of Christianity. Indeed, one fundamentalist Baptist minister told me recently that to become a minister, you do not have to go to school at all, and when you study, you study only the Bible (without learning the languages in which it was written) and "nothing" of the history of theology—which really amounts to *projecting onto* the Bible, not studying it.

No Separation of Church and State

American Protestant fundamentalists insist that America is a Christian nation in spite of the fact that our Constitution expressly separates church and state and our citizens are a great mixture of peoples—Jews, Muslims, Buddhists, Hindus, Native Americans, Christians, atheists, and just plain nonbelievers.

Randall Terry, founder of Operation Rescue and a close friend of the Roman Catholic archbishops of New York and Philadelphia, both of whom were appointed by Cardinal Ratzinger and who agree with Terry's aggressive attacks on abortion clinics, says: "America should function as a Christian nation." But his version of Christianity is one not of love or justice, but of hatred. He declares: "I want you to just let a wave of intolerance wash over you. I want you to let a wave of hatred wash over you. Yes, hate is good . . . Our goal is a Christian nation. We have a biblical duty, we are called by God, to conquer this country. We don't want equal time. We don't want pluralism" (The *News-Sentinel,* Fort Wayne, Indiana, August 16, 1993).

Ralph Reed, executive director of the Christian Coalition, spelled out the Coalition's goal in 1990 when he declared that "[w]hat Christians have got to do is to take back this country, one precinct at a time, one neighborhood at a time and one state at a time . . . I honestly believe that in my lifetime we will see a country once again governed by Christians . . . and Christian values" (Religious News Service, May 15, 1990).

Conservative Paul Weyrich, founder of the Free Congress Research and Education Foundation, states in an October 1995 article in *Freedom Writer:* "[T]he real enemy is the secular humanist" world. Pat Robertson, the top spokesperson for the theocratic wing of the Republican party and long a vocal member of the Christian right, agrees. In November 1991, in comments to the Christian Coalition's "Road to Victory" gathering in Virginia Beach, Virginia, quoted in *Freedom Writer* (January/February 1992), he said that "it's going to be a spiritual battle." Among the members of the "secular left" he decries are: the National Organization for Women, the National Education Association, the National Council of Churches, the Gay-Lesbian Caucus, People For the American Way, and Americans United for Separation of Church and State. The Christian Coalition, which he founded, promotes the agenda of the theocratic right and ranks the members of Congress as to whether they are on board or not. Currently, it gives a 100 percent rating to forty-one of the fifty-one Republican senators and a rating of zero to thirty-one of forty-eight Democrats and to one Independent. Robertson has had a profound effect on American politics in our lifetime.

In a speech at the Maranatha Campus Ministries Convention in Dallas in December, 1984, which was also excerpted in the publication *Fundamentalist Preacher*, Robertson offers this vision: "Every means of communication, the news, the television, the radio, the cinema, the arts, the government, the finance—it's going to be ours! God's going to give it to His people. We should prepare to reign and rule with Jesus Christ." No one can say that the fundamentalist agenda is hidden. It is now out in the open.

Perhaps Robertson's most telling observation can be found in his book *The Millennium* (Dallas: Word Publishing Group, 1990): "With the apathy that exists today, a well organized minority can influence the selection of candidates to an astonishing degree." Apathy does reign, and a tiny theocratic movement has taken over a national party and has rejected the basic tenets of the founding of the United States.

The fundamentalist agenda rejects the Constitution of the United States, in which church and state are purposely kept separate. Pat Robertson, once a candidate for president, declared in an address to the American Center for Law and Justice in Columbia, North Carolina, on November 14, 1993: "There is no such thing as separation of church and state in the Constitution. It is a lie of the Left and we are not going to take it anymore." House Majority leader Tom DeLay offered his interpretation of the Constitution as well when he stated in a speech at a luncheon organized by the televangelist D. James Kennedy at the Center for Christian Statesmanship on July 10, 2001: "[T]his notion of separation of church and state that has been imposed upon us over the last 40 or 50 years. . . . I don't believe there is a separation of church and state. I think the Constitution is very clear."

Reverend Jerry Falwell, so often a guest on *Larry King Live* and other mainstream media broadcasts and who is on the record for having declared on national television "I think Muhammad was a terrorist . . ." (*60 Minutes*, October 6,

2002), has spoken to the application of fundamentalist goals in education: "The public school system is damned . . . put your child in Christian schools. If you can't afford it, homeschool" (from a speech called "Trends in Christian Higher Education," given at Regent University, Virginia Beach, Virginia, September 22, 1993). He also states, in his 1979 book *America Can Be Saved!* (Murfreesboro, Tenn.: Sword of the Lord Publishers, 1979): "I hope to see the day when, as in the early days of our country, we won't have any public schools. The churches will have taken them over again and Christians will be running them. What a happy day that will be." Pat Buchanan, himself a regular on mainstream television talk shows, agrees. As a presidential candidate, he addressed an anti-gay rally in Des Moines on February 11, 1996: "We're going to bring back God and the Bible and drive the gods of secular humanism right out of the public schools of America."

Vengeance from the Punitive Father God

Fundamentalists believe they know who is responsible for evil in the world, including the tragedy of the 9/11 attacks on New York City and Washington, and that vengeance is ours (not the Lord's, as the Bible says). Conservative ideologue Ann Coulter, who for some strange reason appears regularly on national television programs, declares: "We should invade their (Islamic) countries, kill their leaders and convert them to Christianity. We weren't punctilious

about locating and punishing only Hitler and his top offi-
cers. We carpet-bombed German cities, we killed civilians.
That's war. And this is war" (Ann Coulter, "This Is War,"
Universal Press Syndicate, September 14, 2001). Surely
this is the Punitive Father religion at its most intense.

On *The 700 Club* (September 13, 2001), Jerry Falwell
and Pat Robertson discussed the matter after the attacks
and offered their take on the reasons for the tragedy:

Jerry Falwell: And, I know that I'll hear from them
for this. But, throwing God out successfully with the help
of the federal court system, throwing God out of the public square, out of the schools. The abortionists have got to
bear some burden for this because God will not be mocked.
And when we destroy 40 million little innocent babies, we
make God mad. I really believe that the pagans, and the
abortionists, and the feminists, and the gays and the lesbians who are actively trying to make that an alternative
lifestyle, the ACLU, People for the American Way, all of
them who have tried to secularize America. I point the fin-
ger in their face and say "you helped this happen."

Pat Robertson: Well, I totally concur, and the problem
is we have adopted that agenda at the highest levels of our
government. And so we're responsible as a free society for
what the top people do. And the top people, of course, is
the court system.

JF: Amen. Pat, did you notice yesterday? The ACLU,
and all the Christ-haters, People For the American Way,
NOW, etc., were totally disregarded by the Democrats and

the Republicans in both houses of Congress as they went out on the steps and called out to God in prayer and sang "God Bless America" and said "let the ACLU be hanged." In other words, when the nation is on its knees, the only normal and natural and spiritual thing to do is what we ought to be doing all the time—calling upon God.

PR: Amen.

Radio host Rush Limbaugh also believes in a Punitive Father-God who lays down laws in black-and-white absolutes. In his view, this is the only possible conception of the Christian Deity. "[T]he religious left in this country hates and despises the God of Christianity and Catholicism and whatever else. They despise it because they fear it, because it's a threat, because that God has moral absolutes. That God has right and wrong, that God doesn't deal in nuance, that God doesn't deal in gray area, that God says, 'This is right and that is wrong'" (*The Rush Limbaugh Show*, April 27, 2005).

As we've seen in chapter 2, a Punitive Father does not think well of women, who, according to those who subscribe to this deity, are to be blamed for everything from the destruction of the family to the events of 9/11, especially if they are feminists. Pope Benedict XVI, in fact, attacks feminism and what he terms "radical feminism" without defining either of these terms. In a fundraising letter serving as an in-kind contribution to the Iowa Committee of Stop ERA in the summer of 1992 (and reported in the *Washington Post*, August 23. 1993), Pat Robertson declared that the "feminist agenda is not about equal rights for women. It is about a socialist, antifamily political movement that encourages women to leave their husbands, kill their children, practice witchcraft, destroy capitalism and become lesbians." Similarly, he has said on *The 700 Club* (December 3, 1997): "NOW [National Organization for Women] is saying that in order to be a woman, you've got to be a lesbian," and (on April 9, 1991) that Planned Parenthood "is teaching kids to fornicate, teaching people to have adultery, every kind of bestiality, homosexuality, lesbianism—everything that the Bible condemns."

According to religious fundamentalists, liberals too are to expect the vengeance of the Punitive God and his surrogates. On February 2, 2002, Ann Coulter spoke to the Conservative Political Action Conference in Crystal City, Virginia on the subject of the punishment that should be meted out to captured American Taliban member John Walker Lindh: "When contemplating college liberals, you really regret once again that John Walker is not getting the death penalty. We need to execute people like John Walker in order to physically intimidate liberals, by making them realize that they can be killed, too. Otherwise, they will turn out to be outright traitors." Her words received a standing ovation.

Carrying on her crusade in the name of punitive religion and the mingling of politics and God, in an August 20, 2002, interview in the *New York Observer*, Coulter proposed that the *New York Times* building be destroyed just as the government building in Oklahoma City was destroyed: "My only regret with Timothy McVeigh is he did not go to the *New York Times* Building."

Homosexuals will also be avenged by the Punitive Father religion. Underlining her view, Coulter opined in a February 10, 2002 *New York Observer* article: "There's a reason hurricanes are named after women and homosexual men. It's one of our little methods of social control."

The Fundamentalist Apocalypse

Broadcast journalist and commentator Bill Moyers responded to the scary tone of the fundamentalist agenda in a talk at Harvard Medical School on December 1, 2004:

> One of the biggest changes in politics in my lifetime is that the delusional is no longer marginal. It has come in from the fringe, to sit in the seat of power in the Oval Office and in Congress. For the first time in our history, ideology and theology hold a monopoly of power in Washington. Theology asserts propositions that cannot be proven true; ideologues hold stoutly to a worldview despite being contradicted by what is generally accepted as reality. When ideology and theology couple, their offspring are not always bad, but they are always blind. And there is the danger: Voters and politicians alike, oblivious to the facts.

The *Left Behind* series, a bestselling series of books in America today that has sold more than sixty million copies, was written by the Christian fundamentalist and religious-right warrior Timothy LaHaye. The strange theology of the series was originally concocted in the nineteenth century by a couple of immigrant preachers who took disparate passages from the Bible and wove them into a narrative. Captivating the imagination of millions of Americans today, the series' contention can be summarized thus: When Israel has completed its occupation of the rest of its "biblical lands," legions of the anti-Christ will attack it, triggering a final showdown in the valley of Armageddon. Jews who have not been converted will be burned and the Messiah will return on clouds for the Rapture. True believers will be lifted out of their clothes and transported to heaven, where, seated next to the right hand of God, they will watch their political and religious opponents suffer plagues of boils, sores, locusts, and frogs during subsequent years of tribulation—this indeed shows the wrath of a Punitive God who damns to a punitive afterlife. According to the series' view, Christian fundamentalists may look upon environmental destruction as a welcome sign of the coming apocalypse.

But as Moyers pointed out in his December 1, 2004, presentation at Harvard Medical School, those who espouse similar views can be found in powerful places in government:

We're not talking about a handful of fringe lawmakers who hold or are beholden to these beliefs. Nearly

37

half the U.S. Congress before the recent election—231 legislators in total; more since the election—are backed by the religious right. Forty-five senators and 186 members of the 108th Congress earned 80 to 100 percent approval ratings from the three most influential Christian right advocacy groups. They include Senate Majority Leader Bill Frist, Assistant Majority Leader Mitch McConnell, Conference Chair Rick Santorum of Pennsylvania, Policy Chair Jon Kyl of Arizona, House Speaker Dennis Hastert [of Illinois], and Majority Whip Roy Blunt [of Missouri].

Fundamentalists own and operate nineteen hundred "Christian" radio stations and 250 "Christian" television stations in the United States. A 2002 *Time*/CNN poll found that 59 percent of Americans believe that the prophecies found in the Book of Revelation are going to come true. Nearly 25 percent think the Bible predicted the 9/11 attacks.

Protestant and Roman Catholic Fundamentalists Linking Up

Catholics have had a fundamentalist pope for more than twenty-five years—first in Pope John Paul II and now in his right-hand man and former chief inquisitor, Pope Benedict XVI (formerly Cardinal Ratzinger).

The papacy has made extra efforts to link Protestantism and Catholicism, especially on such issues as abortion and homosexuality (yet, strangely, not on such subjects such as capital punishment, war in Iraq, or economic and ecological justice). Studies demonstrate that Cardinal Ratzinger, then-head of the Congregation for the Doctrine of the Faith (called the Office of the Holy Inquisition until 1965), was in great part responsible for the election of George Bush as president in 2004. Here is what transpired: President Bush visited the Vatican on June 4, 2004, in the midst of the presidential contest, and complained that the American Catholic bishops were not offering strong enough support in his battle against abortion and gays. One week after his return to the United States, Cardinal Ratzinger's office informed American Catholic bishops that they should deny communion to any Catholic politician who was not publicly against abortion. John Kerry, of course, was a Catholic. The result? Three states—Ohio, Iowa and New Mexico—were decided by the Roman Catholic vote, which was 6 percent more Republican in these states than it had been in any previous election.

This unprecedented interference in American elections by a foreign head of state—and the subsequent alignment of Protestant and Catholic fundamentalist agendas—will surely not go unnoticed when historians document American history of this period.

Fundamentalists and Nature

A leader in today's theocracy movement is R. J. Rushdooney, the father of "dominion theology." He teaches that "*Dominion* is God's principle for man over nature (Gen. 1:28), and for the male in the person of the husband and father in the family (1 Cor. 11:1–5). Dominion or the male's nature and prerogatives is to be found throughout the animal world as a part of God's creation ordinance." In winning a nation to the gospel, he believes the sword as well as the pen must be used. He considers democracy to be a heresy and his goal is to "replace the heresy of democracy with biblical law" (R. J. Rushdooney, *The Institutes of Biblical Law: A Chalcedon Study* [Nutley, N.J.: Craig Press, 1973], 201).

Ann Coulter expressed similar "dominion" sentiments in the following interview from a series of video clips aired on the Fox News broadcast *Hannity and Colmes* on June 22, 2001:

Ann Coulter: I take the biblical idea. God gave us the earth.

Peter Fenn [Democratic strategist]: Oh, OK.

AC: We have dominion over the plants, the animals, the trees.

PF: This is a great idea.

AC: God says, "Earth is yours. Take it. Rape it. It's yours."

PF: Terrific. We're Americans, so we should consume as much of the earth's resources . . .

AC: Yes! Yes.

PF: . . . as fast as we possibly can.

AC: As opposed to living like the Indians.

Roman Catholic Fundamentalism and the Case of Father Maciel

Roman Catholic fundamentalism is not so much about the authority of the Bible as it is about the authority of the Church. Whether the Church or the Bible, however, what fundamentalism always boils down to is *authority*, for that is the agenda of the Punitive Father.

During the recent and long reign of Pope John Paul II, while the press fawned and salivated over his many public pilgrimages, things were not so pretty back at Vatican headquarters, where one man—Cardinal Ratzinger, now Pope Benedict XVI—was in charge.

For twenty-three years Ratzinger hid in the dark sanctums dedicated to the Inquisition (with the new, less menacing name of the Congregation for the Doctrine of the Faith), expelling more than one hundred Catholic theologians from their teaching assignments and many from their religious or priestly orders and writing documents for Pope John Paul II that were ugly in their tone toward homosexuals, Buddhists, yoga practitioners, and nature lovers and completely ignorant of current science. Now he can no longer hide. The media spotlight will reveal the corruption of this man and a system that not only has appointed every bishop for the past twenty-five years, but that escorted many of them, especially American bishops, through his office for special training.

This is the first time in history that an inquisitor general has been made pope. It is nothing short of a coup d'eglise. Now in the position of pope is the man most responsible for the dumbing down of the clergy and the closing down of theological tradition, the man who claims to be the only one who knows Catholic tradition. A professor from my alma mater, the Institut Catholique de Paris, told me a few years ago that the Vatican had effectively shut down all theological thinking in Catholic universities in Europe. According to some within the Church, the Roman Catholic Church of Pope John Paul II was in schism. It was out of step with the tradition of the *magisterium* (the teaching office of the Catholic Church, which has never been one and the same with the pope) and with episcopal appointments and the teachings of Vatican II regarding collegiality, among other issues.

As more information comes to light regarding priestly pedophilia and subsequent cover-ups undertaken at the highest levels of Church hierarchy, we will come to see that the corruption of the Borgia papacy during the time of Luther's Reformation pales in comparison to the corruption of the papacies of John Paul II and Benedict XVI. Chilling is the fact that the new pope himself refused for twenty years to look into allegations written and testified to by nine victims of Father Marcial Maciel of Mexico, the Vatican-favored priest and founder of Legionaires for Christ, a movement in the Church that was one of the favorite orders of John Paul II.

In the important investigative study *Vows of Silence: The Abuse of Power in the Papacy of John Paul II* (New York: Free Press, 2004), Jason Berry and Gerald Renner, both Catholic journalists with no anti-Catholic bias to project, laid bare what has increasingly proved to be a frightening papacy. Cardinal Ratzinger, it turns out, played a key role in all of its cover-ups. The authors deal at length with Father Maciel and his order, then known as the Legion of Christ. Among other things, the order "cultivated officials in Argentina and Chile, where torture was a part of political strategy." Maciel appealed to fundamentalist Catholics who were the wealthy of Latin America—those who, like Cardinal Ratzinger, were threatened by Liberation Theology's "preferential option for the poor." The Legion of Christ preferred instead a preferential option for the rich and powerful and became known by outsiders as "millionaires for Christ."

Maciel was born in 1920 in a town 220 miles west of Mexico City. In the course of his religious training, he was expelled from two seminaries, after which he started his own. He admired the Spanish dictator and fascist Francisco Franco, as Berry and Renner indicate: "Wealthy Mexicans,

Venezuelans, and Spaniards in Mexico were impressed by Maciel's plan for a corps of priests trained as educators in a quasi-military environment. . . . Maciel created a cult of adoration to himself, 'Nuestro Padre.'" He was a master fundraiser among the rich and connected, and "[i]n raising funds he stressed the order's obedience to the pope"

By all accounts, he also sexually abused many of the young seminarians in his charge. Nine of them have come forward as adults to testify to the abuse they experienced at his hands as young people. One of them tried to bring this mistreatment to the attention of Vatican officials in 1976, 1978, and 1989, but to little avail. To the traditional vows of poverty, obedience, and chastity, Maciel's cult of personality added: Never speak ill of "Nuestro Padre" and spy on anyone who does. Self-flagellation was part of the "spiritual practice" under Maciel. Indeed, years later, one seminarian described Maciel's God in a way that casts him as the classic Punitive Father: He was portrayed as "an implacable being who will throw us into the flames of hell if we died in mortal sin." In Maciel's order, mortal sin included masturbation.

In Berry and Renner's book, one former seminarian tells how, when he was fourteen years old, Maciel (who was also addicted to drugs) took him to his room and forced the boy to masturbate him. In this seminarian's account of his subsequent life, he says: "After being a happy child, I became an introverted, negative young man with fears [and] feelings of guilt [and was] constantly depressed . . .

[I was reminded] of Maciel's threats of hell." His brother, too, was sexually abused by Maciel. Again, he testifies to Maciel's promulgation of the idea of a Punitive Father: "As sons of a Christian family, as Mexicans, we had been taught that the father should be obeyed. Leaving seminary meant eternal damnation. . . . It was a vindictive God." He left the seminary at age twenty-six and later married.

As adults, years after they experienced their abuse and after learning of Pope John Paul II's complimentary words about Maciel and the pontiff's encouragement of his order in the name of "evangelization" in the Church, some of the priest's victims went to the Vatican to blow the whistle on the Mexican priest. Pope John Paul II had given Maciel special attention; the priest accompanied the pontiff on trips to America and elsewhere. *Vows of Silence* is very clear about the pope's relationship to Maciel and his order: "John Paul saw the Legionaires as a sign of Catholic restoration in Latin America, akin to Opus Dei in Spain." He liked "their cultivation of traditional Catholics, their ability to raise funds, and their stance against moral relativism." Along with Opus Dei, the politics of Legionaires for Christ was to take the place of Liberation Theology and base communities, movements that Cardinal Ratzinger and Pope John Paul II, along with the CIA, decimated in Latin America.

The case brought against Maciel by the ex-seminarians ultimately landed in Cardinal Ratzinger's office, which pursued no action over a several-year period. Ratzinger asked whether it was "prudent" to prosecute a priest who had done so much for the Church. Footage in a May 2002 report on ABC's *20/20* showed Ratzinger slapping the hand of Brian Ross, the reporter who had asked him about the Maciel case. So too, Pope John Paul II has been photographed or filmed in the papal airplane giving Maciel a fraternal kiss. As reported in *Vows of Silence,* one of the victims, asked in 2001 about Ratzinger's handling of the canonical case, responded simply, "It is an immoral thing." The canon lawyer under Ratzinger who sheltered Maciel and demanded "professional secrecy" for accused clergy was ultimately named the archbishop of Genoa and was made a cardinal in October 2003.

Sad to say, the investigation of Father Maciel, which was opened in December 2004, was closed in May 2005 by Pope Benedict XVI. This was the first major case of sexual abuse to be considered—and closed—by the new pope.

Frank Keating, a Roman Catholic and former governor of Oklahoma, named chairman of the American bishop's National Review Board, formed to investigate charges of priestly pedophilia after the scandals in this country emerged, commented on his experience after quitting his post (from *Vows of Silence*, 305):

> The American Catholic Church faces a seismic upheaval, and the Catholic lay community is angry and getting angrier. Dioceses are paying huge sums of lay money to settle cases. Recently, the attorney general of Massachusetts—himself a Catholic—writing of the

Boston archdiocese, declared that the mistreatment of children there was "so massive and so prolonged that it borders on the unbelievable."

These kinds of abuses and their cover-up are what happens when you replace theology with ideology. Any potential leadership is dumbed down, which has lead to the worldwide dumbing down and corruption of Church hierarchy during the papacy of John Paul II and now under the rule of Pope Benedict XVI. As the historian Lord Acton observed following the declaration of the doctrine of papal infallibility by the First Vatican Council in 1870: "Power corrupts and absolute power corrupts absolutely."

Father Tom Doyle, a canon lawyer and Dominican who was once groomed by both Rome and the apostolic delegate in Washington, D.C., to climb up the ecclesial ladder, did attempt to blow the whistle on the many abuses of the Church during the papacy of John Paul II. Despite his high status in the Church, Father Doyle eventually woke up to the cover-ups and hypocrisy carried out in the pope's name, and he worked hard to get American bishops to respond to the threat of clerical abuse. In a speech to a gathering of the Voice of the Faithful, a Boston-based organization formed in response to the abuse crisis in the Archdiocese of Boston, he said, as quoted in *Vows of Silence*: "What we have experienced in our lifetime is a disaster the horror of which is perhaps equaled by the bloodshed of the Inquisition, but which certainly makes the indulgence scam that caused the

Reformation pale by comparison. The deadliest symptom is the unbridled addiction to power . . ."

The implementation of a Punitive Father theology has probably not been stronger in the Roman Catholic Church at any time since the days of the Inquisition. The Church's commitment to this theology was obvious during the papacy of John Paul II, when the hierarchy offered unabashed support to Father Maciel and his Legionaires, Father Josemaría Escrivá and Opus Dei, and the right-wing Communion and Liberation movement. This Italian organization was especially loved by Pope John Paul II. It is militantly anti-communist and its followers have been called "the pope's Rambos." Deeply involved in Italian right-wing politics and business, it teaches that a conspiracy of Protestants, communists, secular humanists, liberal Jesuits, and progressive political parties exists to sell out true Christianity—which they equate with that of the Middle Ages. The late pope made them a "secular Institute," which means they can operate in any diocese in the world without the bishop's permission. Pope Benedict XVI also supports them strongly.

"A power structure that is accountable only to itself will always end by abusing the powerless," comments James Carroll, the *Boston Globe* op-ed columnist, in his book *Toward a New Catholic Church: The Promise of Reform* (Boston: Houghton Mifflin, 2002). Say the authors of *Vows of Silence*: "The abuse of power in this papacy has done incalculable damage to pastors, local priests who preach the Word in what they say *and choose not to say*—about birth control, theological justice, and the celibacy law, especially. Most Catholics do not believe the Church on these matters. Ratzinger's demand for 'submission of will' to Rome cannot coexist with the *sensus fidelium*, 'the sense of the faithful.'"

Regarding the evolution of the Catholic Church in light of contemporary worldviews, Pope Benedict XVI has warned against a "dictatorship of relativism." Yes, he knows dictatorships; in fact, he admires them. As Cardinal Ratzinger, his unbridled embrace of Franco's favored priest, Josemaría Escrivá, and his push for Escrivá's canonization demonstrate this pope's knowledge and love of autonomous power. He wants the papacy to be a dictatorship, and aiming for this has been his life's work. For him, papal infallibility buttresses everything the pope says.

It is telling to look closely at the content of the speech Ratzinger made that won him election to the papacy. Traditionally, of course, cardinals are not to "run" for the office of pope, but never being one to be stopped by tradition, Ratzinger has made over these rules. In fact, contrary to all precedent, he even published a book on the eve of the papal election. It was in his speech prior to his election that he offered his condemnation of the "dictatorship of relativism." Yet he does not answer to the dictatorship of absolutism and the dictatorship of Rome, the Inquisition, and the papacy.

As for relativism and relativity, Pope Benedict XVI

seems not to have heard of Albert Einstein. We live in a universe of relativity. Time and space are relative—and curved. We live in a world of inter-relationship, which means that relativity is at the heart of all reality. Relativity is what introduces choice into morality. If all were clear and absolute, there would be no doubts and no choices to make.

Pope Benedict, you cling to absolutism because your faith lies only in man-made, rigid dogmas to which you believe only you hold the key. Rather than trusting, you fear and spread fear in others, demanding "obedience" with loyalty oaths. Your true fear is of chaos itself. You believe that you must bring law and order to a chaotic world that includes women and sex and gays and lesbians and creativity and even thinking theologians. In contrast to your exclusions, Native Americans pray for "all our relations."

Yes, relativity is about "all our relations," all our relatives—which includes our gay relatives. I received the following letter from a gay priest in England, Father Bernard Lynch, who was upset about the recent papal election. His words define the price paid by many groups under a Punitive Father:

> The election of Cardinal Ratzinger to the office of the papacy as Pope Benedict XVI fills me with deep concern as a gay man and Catholic priest. In fact, I believe that if I don't speak, "the very stones themselves will cry out."

The fact remains that Pope John Paul II did lesbian, gay, transgendered, and bisexual peoples untold harm. His writings and his teachings promulgated and proclaimed by Cardinal Ratzinger as head of the Congregation for the Doctrine of the Faith saw our struggle and us not only worthy of condemnation, but as some kind of sinister plot to undermine the very foundations of civilization itself. If the truth were told, the present Pope Benedict XVI and John Paul, in their continuous and consistent rejection of our struggle for equality, tried to rob us of our very souls. I bore first-hand witness to this in my twenty-four years of priestly ministry to gay men suffering and dying from HIV/AIDS. Again and again during the eighties and nineties, at the very height of the pandemic in New York primarily, and then in London, it was my pain and privilege to hold the hand of young Catholic gay men in their twenties and thirties and try to reassure them that they were not condemned to eternal damnation because of what their Church taught about their orientation and their loving sexual behavior. [These were] men too young to have imagined their lives, never mind their deaths. Young people [who] we hear "the Pope loved" [but who were] on the edge of despair as they went to meet their God, because of what the Holy Father, through the Congregation for the Doctrine of the Faith, taught in the name of Christ.

There is no God worth believing in, to my mind,

[who] would so brutally condemn whole multitudes of utterly vulnerable people to such ignominious agony of mind and spirit as they draw their last breath. Most tragically of all for me as a Catholic priest was that at least three of the people I assisted were fellow priests, two of whom, like myself, were Irish-born. Gay men tortured and tormented as they went to meet their Maker by the very Church to whom they had given their lives. Their families and religious communities did not want to know what was happening. This too is the legacy of Pope John Paul and his successor Benedict.

How, one may well ask, can any self-respecting gay man or woman stay within such an oppressive and, in many ways for us, a dehumanizing institution? Many hundreds of thousands of others have understandably walked away. Every single day I think of doing the same. Yet here I am, an openly gay Catholic priest, and still I believe and hope and love from within its ranks.

I do not seek to justify my position either to those on the outside looking in, or [to those on] the inside [who] would willingly give me a one-way ticket out. There is, I believe, no way I can or desire to justify my position to the institutional Church that bears my kind and me such deep disrespect. To even begin to do so would, as I see it, stoop to a level of argument that I have lost even before I begin.

Within the limitations of my knowledge, I understand the Church's reasons for counting me out.

Scripture, tradition, natural law . . . But I am not interested, no matter how plausible their syllogisms or coherent their rhetoric and logic. IT IS NOT GOOD ENOUGH. It is not good enough for any religion that claims to represent the God of the Universe to exclude 10 percent of the peoples of the world from coequality in humanity and in love in the name of that God no matter who his representative is in this time called life.

If God is love—and I absolutely believe He/She is—then we as LGTB peoples are coequally made in the Divine image and have not only the right but the responsibility to live in that love personally, sexually, and spiritually as witness to the fact that love, not power, has the last word. Pope John Paul II was a good and holy human man, but for me and with me, he too was a sinner. It was his sin that blinded him to us as gay people. I pray his successor, Cardinal Ratzinger as Benedict XVI, may have a little more sight. If [he does] not, I shall still go on believing, hoping, and loving until John Paul, Benedict, and I embrace one another as coequals in God, the eternal Lover of all.

What Can We Do?

As we have seen, fundamentalism has taken over much of the Roman Catholic Church and many of the Protestant churches. What theologian Dorothy Soelle has correctly called Christo-fascism is alive and well in Western religion and in some very lofty places in American politics and government.

An alternative is possible, but for this way to be opened, a divorce is necessary. It may be time to let the fundamentalists have the church, with its buildings and museums, its debts and payouts for pedophile offenders. We who believe otherwise and are not fundamentalists will take Christ. And with this simple divorce, a new season may begin: a genuine Pentecost, a rebirth of the church for a third millennium—a church made up of people practicing spirituality, not people structuring a religion. The ninety-five theses that follow shed light on this New Pentecost experience.

This Pentecost will not be fundamentalist and will not be based on worship of a Punitive God. It will not tolerate sexism in itself or those adhering to it. It will worship a God who loves creation and expects us to do the same. It will seek wisdom along with knowledge, a true balance that avoids 1) anti-intellectualism and anti-scientism (as evidenced in the fight against evolution and homosexuality), and 2) rationalism and living and praying in the head. It will honor all the chakras, including the second or sexual chakra, for the sacred energy that can be found in them. See the Song of Songs, a book as holy as any other found in the Bible:

How beautiful you are, my beloved, and how delightful!
All green is our bed . . .

As an apple tree among the trees of the orchards, so is my
    Beloved among the young men . . .
Feed me with raisin cakes,
Restore me with apples, for I am sick with loe.
His left arm is under my head,
His right embraces me. (1.16; 2.3, 5–6)

It will teach meditation forms of many varieties and will empower people to be mystical activists—spiritual warriors, mystics, and prophets.

The new "church" of this New Reformation will have as little structure as possible. As occurred during the years of the early Christian Church, its faithful will meet in people's homes, where the focus will be praying and sharing story—their own and those of others, including that of Jesus. At times—perhaps once a month—they will gather in larger groups to share a true celebration of the larger community, which, with its use of dance and images rather than an overabundance of readings and sermons, will take a form both postmodern and premodern.

Who will lead and be ordained in the church of this New Reformation? The leaders will be those who have trained in the wisdom and creation spirituality tradition (that of the historical Jesus) and who feel called to be part of the leadership of this new church. In keeping with its theology of the *priesthood of all workers*, those who serve will have jobs that are not ecclesial as such. In this new church, rather than being a profession in itself or a privileged hierarchical class, the priesthood will be an avocation, an honoring of the midwifery powers of all workers, for every individual who is doing good work—that is, work that is a blessing to the community—is already a priest, a midwife of grace.

To ensure the inclusion of the whole Western Christian tradition, church leaders will be ordained by several people from a variety of traditions, including the Independent Catholic Church (which maintains what has historically been known as "apostolic succession" and which even Rome has recognized since its emergence from Utrecht after the first Vatican Council). Neither women nor married people nor homosexuals will be excluded from such leadership.

The New Reformation will not be naively unaware of the powers and principalities of this world. Instead, it may take these on directly at times, for it knows that the powers that gather around a Punitive Father ideology—fundamentalism and fascism—are always with us.

This new church, while looking to many spiritual traditions of the past, will trust the Spirit to lead us in new ways for the third millennium. It will understand that we must travel light, divesting ourselves of two thousand years of ecclesial and cultural baggage, for the world today is a new place, crowded and endangered.

This church will be eco-centered, rather than church-centered, for nature—not 150-million-dollar cathedrals—is God's primary temple. It will respect and ask the blessing of the Native American tradition and other indigenous repositories of ancient wisdom. It will honor, not run from the body, which includes paying attention to all seven chakras, with special attention given to the lower chakras that have been so neglected and maligned in the modern era in the West. It will also honor the earth and all her creatures and the Creator of all this beauty.

The new church will know and act on the knowledge that justice and sustainability are one: What is just is sustainable; what is unjust is not sustainable. The huge gap between the world's haves and have-nots is neither just nor sustainable. With creativity and conscience, a new economic system can be birthed—one that works for all, rather than for a privileged few; one that respects the earth and her creatures, rather than vainly pursues money-as-power or money-as-wealth. In fact, the real wealth is to be found in the earth itself.

This Historic Moment

A historic moment is upon us— one just as decisive as that inaugurated by the monk Martin Luther, who responded to Church corruption and theological laziness in the sixteenth century; or by Francis of Assisi, who stood up to institutional dry rot and religious sclerosis in the late twelfth century; or by Benedict, who imagined and birthed an alternative religious lifestyle with his launching of Western monasticism in response to sixth-century imperial ambitions of the Church and barbarian pressures; or that inaugurated by Jesus and Paul, who were inspired to stand up to the Roman Empire and its religions and to re-imagine the Jewish tradition in the first century.

Today ecological crises, poverty crises in the midst of plenty, youth crises, religious crises, educational crises, survival crises, and the worldwide spread of fundamentalist and Punitive Father religiosity require a spiritual awakening at least as great as those in any of those previous periods of history.

It is evident that the organized church and institutional religion are not capable of providing what is needed. What we need today is a Great Awakening, a Great Turning, as the eco-philosopher and deep ecology scholar Joanna Macy puts it. This awakening is possible and within our reach. Interfaith identity has never been more possible and alive. Yes, the biggest obstacle to it is, as the Dalai Lama teaches, a bad relationship with our own faith traditions. The theses in this book are offered as a means of renewing the faith tradition of the West. New scholarship and discoveries in archaeology—which include the "lost" books of Christianity's origins—lend credence to this awakening. Monks today, living away from monasteries and among the people, teach us ways to meditate and calm the reptilian brain. The Internet and the media provide both information and the rapid communication of ideas. Awareness of the ineffectiveness of our basic institutions of education, economics, politics, and religion is visible everywhere.

The fact that the ancient Roman Catholic Church can do no better than elect as pope the man who resuscitated the Inquisition is proof that institutional religion is in need of a complete overhaul. A return to the prophets and mystics and the gospels is imperative, as it was in the days of Luther or Francis or Benedict or Jesus himself. Great individuals of the twentieth century, from Gandhi and Martin Luther King Jr. and Howard Thurman to Dorothy Day and Oscar Romero and many others, have shown us the way, which is within our grasp. We must seize this Pentecostal moment.

Pentecost, often called the birthday of the Church, must be understood today as the rebirth of the church—of Christianity and of all our faiths. We must clear from all religion the Punitive Father God, the fundamentalist God, and we must allow the return of the Divine Feminine, for both it and the truly Sacred Masculine are integral to any faith. For centuries, a pseudo-Sacred Masculine has been ruling the world. Patriarchy, with its commitment to war and control, fear of chaos, fear of nature, fear of body, fear of women, fear of homosexuals, fear of "the other," has ruled long enough. "Love drives out fear," says John's Epistle. Love must replace fear, and a Mother–Father God must replace an all-male deity.

The age of denominationalism—an age that reflected a Newtonian "parts" mentality and nation-state boxes—is decisively over. Independence is giving way to interdependence. Christianity is one *and* diverse. Spirituality is one *and* diverse. The future of humankind lies in sharing of the wisdom of all the world's spiritual traditions.

4

95 Theses or Articles of Faith for a Christianity for the Third Millennium

Like Martin Luther before me, I present here ninety-five theses—or faith observations. These have been drawn from my sixty-five years of living and practicing religion and spirituality. I trust I am not alone in recognizing these truths. For me they represent a return to our origins, to the spirit and teachings of Jesus and his prophetic ancestors, and to the Christ unleashed by Jesus' presence and teachings.

These theses are an invitation to discussion and debate. They and the issues raised in this book are about not just a Reformation, but a *transformation*. Can what we know as Christianity transform itself for a new millennium and the generations to come? Can it take from its past only what is wise and move into a new age with a renewed commitment to sustainability for the earth and justice for the earth's people?

1

God is both Mother and Father.

2

At this time in history, God is more Mother than Father because the feminine is most missing and it is important to bring back gender balance.

3

God is always new, always young, and always "in the beginning."

4

God the Punitive Father is not a God worth honoring, but a false god and an idol that serves empire builders. The notion of a punitive, all-male God, is contrary to the full nature of the Godhead, who is as much female and motherly as masculine and fatherly.

5

"All the names we give to God come from an understanding of ourselves" (Meister Eckhart). Thus people who worship a Punitive Father are themselves punitive.

6

—⟫⟪—

Theism (the idea that God is "out there" or above and beyond the universe) is false. All things are in God and God is in all things (*panentheism*).

7

—⟫⟪—

Everyone is born a mystic and a lover who experiences the unity of things, and all are called to keep alive this mystic or lover of life.

8

All are called to be prophets, which is to interfere with injustice.

9

Wisdom is love of life. (See the Book of Wisdom, "This is wisdom: to love life," and Christ in John's Gospel: "I have come that you may have life and have it in abundance.")

10

God loves all of creation, and science can help us more deeply penetrate and appreciate the mysteries and wisdom of God in creation. Science is no enemy of true religion.

11

Religion is not necessary, but spirituality is.

12

"Jesus does not call us to a new
religion, but to life" (Dietrich
Bonhoeffer). Spirituality is living life
at a depth of newness and gratitude,
courage and creativity, trust and letting
go, compassion and justice.

13

Spirituality and religion are not the
same any more than education and
learning, law and justice, or commerce
and stewardship are the same.

14

Christians must distinguish between
God (masculine and history, liberation
and salvation) and Godhead (feminine
and mystery, being and nonaction).

15

Christians must distinguish between
Jesus (a historical figure) and Christ
(the experience of God-in-all-things).

16

Christians must distinguish between Jesus and Paul.

17

Jesus, not unlike many spiritual teachers, taught us that we are sons and daughters of God and are to act accordingly by becoming instruments of divine compassion.

18

Eco-justice is a necessity for planetary survival and human ethics; without it we are crucifying the Christ all over again in the form of destruction of forests, waters, species, air, and soil.

19

Sustainability is another word for justice, for what is just is sustainable and what is unjust is not.

20

A preferential option for the poor,
as found in the base community
movement, is far closer to the teaching
and spirit of Jesus than is a preferential
option for the rich and powerful, as
found, for example, in Opus Dei.

21

Economic justice requires the work
of creativity to birth a system of
economics that is global, respectful
of the health and wealth of the earth
systems, and that works for all.

22

Celebration and worship are key to human community and survival, and such reminders of joy deserve new forms that speak in the language of the twenty-first century.

23

Sexuality is a sacred act and a spiritual experience, a *theophany* (revelation of the Divine), a mystical experience. It is holy and deserves to be honored as such.

24

Creativity is both humanity's greatest gift and its most powerful weapon for evil, and so it ought to be both encouraged *and* steered to humanity's most God-like activity, which all religions agree is compassion.

25

There is a priesthood of all workers (all who are doing good work are midwives of grace and are therefore priests), and this priesthood ought to be honored as sacred and workers should be instructed in spirituality in order to carry on their ministry effectively.

26

Empire-building is incompatible with Jesus' life and teaching and with Paul's life and teaching and with the teaching of holy religions.

27

Ideology is not *theology*; ideology endangers the faith because it replaces thinking with obedience and distracts from the responsibility of theology to adapt the wisdom of the past to today's needs. Instead of thinking, it demands loyalty oaths to the past.

28

Loyalty is not a sufficient criterion
for ecclesial office—intelligence and
proven conscience are.

29

No matter how much the television
media fawn over the pope and papacy
because it makes good theater, the
pope is not the Church but has a
ministry within the Church. *Papalolotry*
is a contemporary form of idolatry and
must be resisted by all believers.

30

Creating a Church of sycophants
is not a holy thing. Sycophants
(*Webster's Dictionary* defines them
as "servile, self-seeking flatterers")
are not spiritual people, for their
only virtue is obedience. A society
of sycophants—sycophant clergy;
sycophant seminarians; sycophant
bishops; sycophant cardinals;
sycophant religious orders of Opus
Dei, Legionaires for Christ, and
Communion and Liberation; and the
sycophant press—do not represent in
any way the teachings or the person of
the historical Jesus, who chose to stand
up to power rather than amassing it.

31

Vows of pontifical secrecy are a certain way to corruption and cover-up in the Church, as in any human organization.

32

Original Sin is an ultimate expression of a Punitive Father God and is not a biblical teaching. But Original Blessing (goodness and grace) is biblical.

33

The term *original wound* better describes the separation humans experience on leaving the womb and entering the world—a world that is often unjust and unwelcoming—than does the term Original Sin.

34

Fascism and the compulsion to control are not the paths of peace or compassion, and those who practice fascism are not fitting models for sainthood. The seizing of the apparatus of canonization to canonize fascists is a stain on the Church.

35

The Spirit of Jesus and other prophets calls people to simple lifestyles in order that "the people may live."

36

Dance, whose root meaning in many indigenous cultures is the same as *breath* or *spirit*, is a very ancient and appropriate form in which to pray.

37

To honor the ancestors and celebrate
the communion of saints does not mean
putting heroes on pedestals, but rather
honoring them by living out lives of
imagination, courage, and compassion
in our own time, culture, and historical
moment, as they did in theirs.

38

A diversity of interpretation of the
Jesus event and the Christ experience is
altogether expected and welcome, as it
was in the earliest days of the Church.

39

Therefore *unity* of church does not mean *conformity*. There is unity in diversity. Coerced unity is not unity.

40

The Holy Spirit is perfectly capable of working through participatory democracy in church structures; hierarchical and dominating modes of operating can indeed interfere with the work of the Spirit.

41

The body is an awe-filled, sacred
Temple of God. This does not mean
it is untouchable, but rather that each
of its dimensions, well-named by the
seven chakras, is as holy as the others.

42

Thus our connection with the earth
(first chakra) is holy; and our sexuality
(second chakra) is holy; and our moral
outrage (third chakra) is holy; and
our love that stands up to fear (fourth
chakra) is holy; and our prophetic
voice that speaks out (fifth chakra) is
holy; and our intuition and intelligence
(sixth chakra) are holy; and our gifts
we extend to the community of light
beings and ancestors (seventh chakra)
are holy.

43

The prejudice of rationalism and the left brain, located in the head, must be balanced by attention to the lower chakras as equal places for wisdom and truth and Spirit to act.

44

The central chakra, compassion, is the test of the health of all the others, which are meant to serve it, for "by their fruits you will know them" (Jesus).

45

"Joy is the human's noblest act" (Thomas Aquinas). Are our culture and its professions, education, and religion, promoting joy?

46

The human psyche is made for the cosmos and will not be satisfied until the two are reunited and awe, the beginning of wisdom, results from this reunion.

47

The four paths named in the creation
spiritual tradition more fully name the
mystical/prophetic spiritual journey
of Jesus and the Jewish tradition
than do the three paths of purgation,
illumination, and union, which do not
derive from the Jewish and biblical
tradition.

48

Thus it can be said that God is
experienced through ecstasy, joy,
wonder, and delight (*via positiva*).

49

God is experienced through darkness,
chaos, nothingness, suffering, silence,
and in learning to let go and let be
(*via negativa*).

50

God is experienced through acts
of creativity and co-creation
(*via creativa*).

51

All people are born creative. It
is spirituality's task to encourage
holy imagination, for all are born
in the "image and likeness" of the
Creative One, and "the fierce power
of imagination is a gift from God"
(Kabbalah).

52

If you can talk, you can sing; if you can
walk, you can dance (African proverb).
If you can talk, you are an artist
(Native American saying).

53

God is experienced in our struggle for justice, healing, compassion, and celebration (*via transformativa*).

54

The Holy Spirit works through all cultures and all spiritual traditions; it "blows where it will" and is not the exclusive domain of any one tradition and never has been.

55

God speaks today, as in the past, through all religions and all cultures and all faith traditions, none of which is perfect and an exclusive avenue to truth, but all of which can learn from each other.

56

Therefore, an interfaith identity or deep ecumenism are necessary parts of spiritual praxis and awareness in our time.

57

Since the number one obstacle to an interfaith identity is "a bad relationship with one's own faith" (the Dalai Lama), it is important that Christians know their own mystical and prophetic tradition, one that is larger than a religion of empire and its Punitive Father images of God.

58

The cosmos is God's holy temple and our holy home.

59

Fourteen billion years of evolution and unfolding of the universe bespeak the intimate sacredness of all that *is*.

60

All that is is holy and all that is is related, for all being in our universe began as one being just before the fireball erupted.

61

Interconnectivity is not only a
law of physics and of nature, but
also forms the basis of community
and compassion. Compassion is
the working out of our shared
interconnectivity, both as to our shared
joy and our shared suffering
and struggle for justice.

62

The universe does not suffer from a
shortage of grace, and no religious
institution is to see its task as rationing
grace. Grace is abundant in God's
universe.

63

Creation, incarnation, and resurrection are continuously happening on a cosmic as well as a personal scale. So too are life, death, and resurrection (regeneration and reincarnation) happening on a cosmic scale as well as a personal one.

64

Biophilia, or love of life, is everyone's daily task.

65

Necrophilia, or love of death, is to be opposed in self and society in all its forms.

66

Evil can happen through every people, every nation, every tribe, and every individual human, and so vigilance and self-criticism and institutional criticism are always called for.

67

Not all who call themselves Christian
deserve that name just as "not all
who say 'Lord, Lord' shall enter the
kingdom of heaven" (Jesus).

68

Pedophilia is a terrible wrong, but its
cover-up by hierarchy is even more
despicable.

69

Loyalty and obedience are never greater virtues than conscience and justice.

70

Jesus said nothing about condoms, birth control, or homosexuality.

71

A church that is more preoccupied with sexual wrongs than with wrongs of injustice is itself sick.

72

Since homosexuality is found among
464 species and in 8 percent of
any given human population, it is
altogether natural, for those who are
born that way are a gift from God and
nature to the greater community.

73

Homophobia in any form is a serious
sin against love of neighbor, a sin
of ignorance of the richness and
diversity of God's creation, and a sin of
exclusion.

74

Racism, sexism, and militarism are also serious sins.

75

Poverty for the many and luxury for the few are not right or sustainable.

76

Consumerism is today's version of gluttony and needs to be confronted by creating an economic system that works for all peoples and all earth's creatures.

77

Seminaries as we know them, with their excessive emphasis on left-brain work, often kill and corrupt the mystical soul of the young instead of encouraging the mysticism and prophetic consciousness that is there. They should be replaced by wisdom schools.

78

Inner work is required of us all. Therefore, spiritual practices of meditation should be available to all, and this helps in calming the reptilian brain. Silence or contemplation and learning to be still can and ought to be taught to all children and adults.

79

Outer work needs to flow from our inner work, just as action flows from nonaction and true action from being.

80

A wise test of right action is this: What is the effect of this action on people seven generations from today?

81

Another test of right action is this: Is what I am doing, is what we are doing, beautiful or not?

82

Eros, the passion for living, is
a virtue that combats *acedia,* or
the lack of energy to begin new
things, also expressed as depression,
cynicism, or sloth (and also known as
couchpotatoitis).

83

The dark night of the soul descends on
us all and the proper response is not
addiction, such as shopping, alcohol,
drugs, TV, sex or religion, but rather to
be with the darkness and learn from it.

84

The dark night of the soul is a learning place of great depth. Stillness is required.

85

Not only is there a dark night of the soul, but also a dark night of society and a dark night of our species.

86

Chaos is a friend and a teacher and an integral part or prelude to new birth. Therefore, it is not to be feared or compulsively controlled.

87

Authentic science can and must be one of humanity's sources of wisdom, for it is a source of sacred awe, childlike wonder, and truth.

88

When science teaches that matter is "frozen light" (physicist David Bohm), it is freeing human thought from scapegoating flesh as something evil and instead reassuring us that all things are light. This same teaching is found in the Christian gospels (Christ is the light in all things) and in Buddhist teaching (the Buddha nature is in all things). Therefore, flesh does not sin; it is our choices that are sometimes off center.

89

The proper objects of the human heart are truth and justice (Thomas Aquinas), and all people have a right to these through healthy education and healthy government.

90

God is only one name for the Divine One; there are an infinite number of names for God and the Godhead, and still God "has no name and will never be given a name" (Meister Eckhart).

91

—⋗⋖—

Three highways into the heart are
silence and love and grief.

92

—⋗⋖—

The grief in the human heart needs to
be attended to by rituals and practices
that, when practiced, will lessen anger
and allow creativity to flow anew.

93

Two highways out of the heart are creativity and acts of justice and compassion.

94

Since angels learn exclusively by intuition, when we develop our powers of intuition, we can expect to meet angels along the way.

95

True intelligence includes feeling,
sensitivity, beauty, the gift of
nourishment, and humor, which is
a gift of the Spirit (paradox being
its sister).

Passing from Modern to Postmodern Religion

What is our moment in history? How do we name what we are undergoing as a species and as a church at this time? Much seems up for grabs. Today, much is unknown. Fear and anxiety are compounded by terrorist events and the spread of nuclear weapons, poverty in the midst of excessive riches, a media that does not offer critical analysis but instead whips people to frenzy for going to war, corruption in religion, the relatively new inventions of the Internet and e-mail and digital music and cameras—so much is happening so fast! Is there a way to name what is going on and to understand our role in a present that is moving at such a pace that, as one scientist says, culture is outstripping evolution as the most powerful force on the planet?

One way to understand the times we live in is to understand the shift that is occurring from *modern* to *postmodern* consciousness. Because many people have their own take on the meaning of *postmodern*, I will spell out explicitly my conception of the term: I equate the beginning of the modern world with the invention of the printing press in the late fifteenth century. Another event of the late fifteenth century was of course Columbus's arrival in the Americas in 1492. His encounter with indigenous peoples unleashed similar actions the world over. Conquest—of native peoples and of nature itself—was part of the modern era from the beginning.

Martin Luther's "revolution" was directly related to the invention of the printing press, as we saw in chapter 1. The dissemination of the Bible and of written knowledge, which became possible thanks to the printing press, begged for a religious response, and the Reformation provided it. The subsequent humanistic movement that called on the wisdom of pre-Christian philosophy and mathematics also fed the origins of the modern era, an age that has given rise to the Enlightenment; the Industrial Revolution; the World Wars of the twentieth century; the insights of science, including the genius of Galileo, Copernicus, Newton, Darwin, and Pasteur, as well as the excesses of that discipline; the imbalanced power of patriarchy in so many forms; the denominationalism of religions; the landing on the moon; and much more.

What mainline Christian churches must recognize is this: They are completely stuck in the modern era, with its seminary system that so ignores the arts, cosmology, and the mystical and with its worship, which is excessively rational and "in the head." Only the fundamentalists have responded to the shift from modern to post-modern religion—but they have done so in a most peculiar manner. From the point of view of electronic media, they are way out front, having purchased thousands of radio stations and dozens of television stations. While many mainline churches do not maintain vast e-mail lists of their members, fundamentalist churches have updated lists galore, allowing them to reach their constituents directly and swiftly.

But in terms of postmodern science and feminism, creation spirituality, deep ecumenism, and rights for sexual minorities, they are saying: "Back to the seventeenth century." Pope Benedict XVI, Pat Robinson, and Jerry Falwell are leading the parade backward to a time when women "knew their place" and believers were to focus on their souls ("Jesus saves") and remain oblivious to science's teachings about God's creation.

Fundamentalists have indeed responded to postmodern times. But though they have seized control of contemporary technological apparatus, their message unfortunately sounds a retreat back to modern times. Meanwhile, mainline churches have been sleeping. But to arouse them is to arouse a sleeping giant. Much can happen when they throw off the diversions created by debates on issues such as homosexuality and focus instead on what really matters. Much can happen when they recover the moral outrage and intellectual depth of their prophetic ancestors. The moment exists for mainline churches to wake up and respond to the postmodern revolution and the renaissance it implies. Perhaps the following chart will assist that movement and understanding.

MODERN CONSCIOUSNESS	POSTMODERN CONSCIOUSNESS
Began with the invention of the printing press	Began with the invention of electronic media
Emphasizes *text*	Emphasizes *context*
Emphasizes words	Emphasizes dance and images
Throws out the past	Conserves some aspects of the past and lets go of others
Focuses on conquest	Focuses on our common survival
Anthropocentric	Ecological/cosmological
Christ is identified exclusively with Jesus	The cosmic Christ and Buddha nature exist in all things
The aesthetic is de-emphasized and is seen as subjective	The aesthetic and the political are basic to a common morality
Innovation conquers tradition	A tension exists between innovation and tradition
Truth is in the head; emphasizes "clear and distinct ideas" (Descartes)	Truth is in the whole body and all the chakras
Anti-mystical	Eager for mysticism
Worshippers sit	Worshippers dance
Form is absolute (mechanical law)	Form evolves
Dismisses premodern wisdom	Eagerly accepts premodern wisdom
Focuses on the part; emphasizes the part rather than the whole	Cosmological; focuses on the whole (cosmos and ecosystems)

MODERN CONSCIOUSNESS	POSTMODERN CONSCIOUSNESS
Operates from denominational identity	Operates from deep ecumenism and interfaith identity
Functions on a tribal model	Functions on a community model
Perspective is either/or	Perspective accepts double coding and a belief that we are interdependent
Fosters separateness	Fosters mixing and honors diversity
Social change involves only external structures	Social change involves both internal psyche and external structures
Embraces religion	Embraces spirituality
Is serious and somber in tone	Recognizes the value of fun and play
Obedience is the prime virtue	Creativity, a law of the universe, is to be imitated
Incorporates objective rules	Incorporates relativity
Institutes rigid and clear boundaries	Acknowledges that boundaries are fading
Resulted in the Protestant Reformation and Catholic Counter-Reformation	Calls for a new Protestant *and* Catholic Reformation that is also a transformation

Because the printing press was so basic to the launching of the modern era, we might say that *text* is what most characterized that age. The postmodern era, however, is more about *context* than *text*. In my view, postmodernism emerged in the 1960s, with the breakdown of the modern era and the rise of electronic media and cybernetics. Architect Charles Jenks has edited a very helpful volume, entitled *The Postmodern Reader,* in which he has gathered essays by a number of thinkers from a variety of disciplines and countries who speak on the meaning of postmodernism. For instance, French philosopher Andreas Huyssen points out that postmodern consciousness is different from both modernism and avant-gardism because "it raises the question of cultural tradition and conservation in the most fundamental way as an aesthetic and a political issue." Interestingly, politics and aesthetics go together at this time. Postmodernism recognizes a "field of tension between tradition and innovation" (page 66). The question has become: What must we conserve and what must we relinquish?

In a postmodern world the issue of the aesthetic as political plays out in religion, especially around forms of worship. Many Westerners are abandoning church attendance because they find formal, institutional worship to be neither participatory nor aesthetically stimulating. Currently, Western liturgy is so strongly linked to the modern worldview that it has become overly rational or "in the head." It is too often word-oriented and text-oriented and oblivious to the body and the physical. A postmodern worship would, in contrast, incorporate the body and lower chakras and employ postmodern electronic imaging, music, and dance.

Surely, today the tension between tradition and innovation is playing out in the religious sphere in other ways as well. For example, Pope Benedict XVI, who represents tradition and refuses all innovation, understands tradition as the past, but not necessarily the living past. He does not acknowledge aspects of the tradition that may have been innovative, such as the role of the goddess during the twelfth-century renaissance or Thomas Aquinas's teachings on abortion. (Aquinas, unlike present-day Catholic Church officials, taught that abortion of a young fetus is not the destruction of a human being because the fetus, at first a vegetative soul and then an animal soul, does not become a human soul until very late in pregnancy.)

We can find the tension between tradition and innovation in religion likewise played out where evolution is condemned by fundamentalist believers and where homosexuality becomes a key issue in church politics ("innovation" being the scientific awareness that 8 to 10 percent of any given human population is homosexual and that homosexual populations have been found in at least 464 other species).

The question of conservation versus letting go in the sphere of modern consciousness has often resulted in throwing the baby out with the bath water. In a postmodern world, the question of what to keep and what to relinquish calls for more refined decision-making.

Interestingly, the issue of conservation versus relinquishing has led to the basic postmodern motifs of deconstruction and reconstruction. Unfortunately, some postmodern academicians have simply wanted to deconstruct or take apart, but have taken no responsibility whatsoever for reconstruction or putting together again. This is profoundly irresponsible; if we are to criticize what is, we must also give birth to forms that can be more nourishing, as has been done with the Cosmic Mass worship services. Having studied and deconstructed the old liturgical form, we have found within it the four paths of creation spirituality, which in turn have given us the basis for a positive and powerful reconstruction. These four paths are the *via positiva* (awe, wonder, delight, and gratitude), the *via negativa* (silence, letting go, grieving), the *via creativa* (creativity), and the *via transformativa* (justice, compassion, celebration). By keeping these basic elements and adding more ancient and premodern forms of prayer such as dance and drum (I recognize electronic music as urban drumming), we have been able to reconstruct a form of worship.

Jenks believes that pluralism is one of the most fundamental elements of postmodern consciousness. He defines pluralism as "the end of a single worldview—a resistance to single explanations, a respect for difference and a celebration of the regional, local and particular" (page 11). Huyssen agrees when he speaks of "a growing awareness that other cultures, non-European, non-Western cultures, must be met by means other than conquest or domination" (page 69). Jenks sees that "an essential goal of the post-modern movement . . . is to further pluralism, to overcome the elitism inherent in the previous paradigm" (page 12). And of course there was an inherent elitism in the modern era, a presumption, for example, that the premodern, indigenous peoples of the world were somehow inferior or ignorant or stupid. But in our postmodern time we are growing to respect the wisdom of premodern peoples. Indeed, in many ways postmodern awareness has more in common with premodern thinking, particularly with its emphasis on the roles of creativity and cosmology.

Regarding the postmodern cosmological view, the late physicist Dave Bohm said: "I am developing a postmodern physics that begins with the whole." The word *cosmology* in fact comes from the Greek word *kosmos*, or "whole." Thus a postmodern religion rediscovers cosmology and with it the cosmic Christ or cosmic wisdom tradition. It also relearns prayer from ancient peoples who never abandoned the bringing together of microcosm and macrocosm and body, mind, and spirit as the basis of ritual. It incorporates into its worship dance and movement more than mere text (as is done in the Cosmic Mass liturgy). In many African languages—as well as in Hebrew—the word for *dance* is the same as the word for *breath*, and the word for *breath* is the same as the word for *spirit*. Postmodern worship and education reject Descartes's teaching that truth is "clear and distinct ideas" and is therefore found exclusively in the head—as if what we feel in our guts, our hearts, our sexuality, our feet, and through our connection to the earth are not also sources of truth.

Another way in which religion responds to the pluralistic aspect of postmodernism is by embracing deep ecumenism and interfaith beliefs. The traditionalists may cry "syncretism," but the reality is that conquest, domination, elitism, and proselytizing all work together as expressions of denominationalism. Those who adopt a postmodern religious awareness see the limits to any single tradition and reach out to others beyond their own not to steal, but to learn from them and, in turn, to purify their own tradition. As Jenks puts it, "Different cultures acknowledge each other's legitimacy. The motives are equally political and aesthetic" (page 13). Likewise, of postmodern ecumenism, we can say that all religions acknowledge each other's legitimacy.

Those who operate with a postmodern consciousness do not throw out all that is modern; instead postmodernism revitalizes the modern, recognizing areas that have not been well served by modern awareness and action. Jenks sees what he calls double-coding as constituting "the fundamental agenda of the postmodern movement." Double-coding is "a strategy of affirming and denying the existing power structures at the same time, inscribing and challenging different tastes and opposite forms of discourse." Modernism tends to think in either/or terms—either you are a Lutheran or a Catholic, a socialist or a capitalist; a Buddhist or a Christian. But double coding is less either/or thinking than an acknowledgment of our interdependence. We are part of the West and can thus affirm the good parts but criticize the bad parts without altogether abandoning the ship.

I see the key word in postmodernism to be *mixing* (a deejay mixes music and a veejay mixes images). Jenks observes that "virtually all postmodern writers mix genres, hence the hybrid subject matter and heterogeneous audiences" (page 15). Mixing is an expression of the pluralism in postmodernism. Deep ecumenism or interfaith structures do lead to mixing, and that is not a bad thing, by any means. Indeed, it is an honoring of diversity and, what's more, it makes things interesting and lively once again. It sparks creativity and, springing in part from postmodernism's acceptance of diversity, it brings to life a kind of optimism that is not at all naïve: It does not sweep evil under the rug; it acknowledges that evil exists and that tragedy is real, but does not succumb to cynicism or to despair. Amidst its awareness of the reality of tragedy, it remains optimistic.

With regard to movements that have taken place in the postmodern world, Jenks sees as key electronic democracy, information-age pluralism, and self-organization. The Civil Rights movement, for instance, was probably the first such postmodern movement, and what made it succeed was television: A critical moment in the struggle was when citizens nationwide saw police dogs attacking citizens in the streets of Alabama. The national consciousness became engaged. Greenpeace has also tapped into the potential of the image:

The story it generated by chasing whale boats in rubber dinghies brought the media into its larger political movement.

Sociologist Walter Truett Anderson recognizes the women's movement as being expressive of the move from modern to postmodern political movements because it mixed politics and psychotherapy, personal change and political change. He observes, "It is hardly surprising, then, that women are deeply involved in every aspect of the postmodern dialogue" (page 141). In the modern worldview, a change in social structures alone is considered adequate, but postmodern social action agenda includes the expectation of psychic as well as social transformation. Psychic and social structures must be addressed at the same time and must change at the same time, for it is the human psyche that builds social structures and that depends on them.

Certainly postmodernism considers playfulness and fun to have great value. "If it ain't fun, don't do it," say some today. We must visit the past with a sense of awareness and irony rather than with innocence, for our innocence is quite lost. Life is really storytelling, and story—including the storytelling of cosmology, which embodies the tales of how we got here—plays an essential part in postmodern communication. Interestingly, the media is especially good at storytelling.

Anderson points out that identity and boundaries are in flux in our postmodern time: "We live in the age of fading boundaries." I have written about being a "post-denominational priest," which means that I, like so many of us, belong to several communities at once. Though now an Episcopalian, I never formally left Catholicism (after fifty-four years, how could I, even if I wanted to?). Anderson observes that we all belong to so many communities at once today that we should write "etc." after our names. Think of it: Each of us has not only a religious background but ethnic roots, a profession, a gender, a gender preference, a nation, a political affiliation, an economic class, a neighborhood, a family—all of which constitute the diversity of communities to which we belong.

What of morality in a postmodern world? Today, morality is found less in books and frozen laws than among caring people who wrestle with the ethical challenges of our time. We may alter our relationships to tradition, custom, and institutions, but we do not feel driven to discard all socially constructed realities just because we recognize them as such.

As for our relationship to premodern realities, Professor Ray Griffen points out that we of the postmodern world honor the premoderns instead of dismissing them as mere savages or as irrelevant. The search for wisdom takes us back as well as forward. Much that the modern worldview ignores—such as our relationships to the earth and to other species and to the universe and to our own creativity—the premoderns took very seriously. We have much to learn from them.

In a brilliant essay on postmodern blackness, philosopher bell hooks (intentionally lowercase) indicates that the bridge between the lowest classes and the intellectual class is aesthetics—our shared love of beauty. (On the other hand, the modern consciousness, typified by Descartes, altogether ignores beauty and aesthetics as a moral or ethical category, and so too does modern theology.) But the next revolution, hooks proposes, will be a revolution in aesthetics. Perhaps worship might lead the way in this rebirth. Surely that has been the intention of the Cosmic Mass during the past nine years it has been practiced.

Given these changes from modern to postmodern consciousness, we now have a context within which to consider the questions raised in this book. Is it time for a new religious Reformation to respond to the move from modern thinking to postmodern thinking, just as the Reformation in Luther's time responded to the move to modern consciousness? Should this New Reformation be so deep that it becomes a true transformation? If so, what guidelines are appropriate for such an awakening? Do these ninety-five theses help us to name the issues at hand? If so, which among them describe our biggest challenges? Are our current institutions capable of carrying through with this Reformation, or do we need new wine skins for this new wine?

Clearly we need postmodern forms of religion for our postmodern times. That only makes sense. Modern consciousness cannot and will not birth such forms. The young—who are citizens of postmodern rather than modern consciousness—do not identify with modern forms of religion (or anything else that is modern). It is interesting that where Christianity is liveliest today—in Africa—it is contextualized by what are essentially premodern forms of worship that include dance and chant. The rave celebrations that the young flock to all over the world are attractive and alluring because they invoke premodern forms of celebration. It is from them that we have borrowed elements for the Cosmic Mass.

The introduction of new forms of worship was an integral part of the Protestant Reformation under Luther. These forms very much connected to the modern invention of the printing press and with it the dissemination of the Bible and musical books to a more literate population. Luther also called for worship in the vernacular languages and for more emphasis on preaching the "Word" of the Bible. So revolutionary was this liturgical renewal that putting a stop to it was the primary motivation leading the Catholic emperor to try to capture and destroy Luther.

Today is another period, another era. Today, too, integral to a New Reformation are new forms of worship. The old forms inherited from the modern era are very often boring and deadly, inviting people to pray only from the neck up while ignoring the lower chakras, much as they are ignored in modern education. The new language of the postmodern era—including electronic music, images, deejays, veejays, rap, the spoken word, and more—can bring new life and deep spirit to worship, by inspiring dance rather than by encouraging sitting.

I know this is true because I have been involved for nine years in incorporating this postmodern language into ancient liturgical forms of worship. The results are powerful not just for young people, but for people of all ages. We have celebrated more than ninety Cosmic Masses in many cities (mostly in Oakland, California) over this nine-year period and are now actively committed to training others to mount these forms of worship and celebration in their communities. In addition, Canadian television has produced a fifteen-minute DVD on the Cosmic Mass. More information is available at www.thecosmicmass.org.

A few years ago, during a workshop I was offering in Florida, I put on some electronic music and invited the participants to dance. Afterward, a sophisticated woman in her forties came up to me with tears on her cheeks, and she told me this story: "I am a practicing Episcopalian," she said, "and I love my faith, but my eleven-year-old boy can't come to church with me. When we even come close to the building, his body shakes all over. This has pained me for a long time: the divorce of my son and me when it comes to religion. But in the middle of this dance a voice came to me and said, 'Here is a way that you and your son can pray together.' Thus, my tears. They are tears of joy." In this woman's words we see what is at stake in moving from modern to postmodern forms of religion: In what language will our children and grandchildren be praying? These are the stakes that call for a New Reformation, a new transformation.

In speaking about Martin Luther and the Reformation

to groups today, I have learned that very few Latino people know about Martin Luther and the Reformation. After all, it occurred in a faraway culture and time. When I watched the DVD of the 2003 MGM film *Luther* with a friend from Central America, he was astonished to hear that five hundred years ago a Catholic monk stood up to the corruption in the Catholic papacy. What's more, he was invigorated and excited about what he had learned. Interestingly, many Latinos would like to see a reform in the Catholic Church of our time—a movement that does not involve the Legionaires of Christ or Opus Dei and that connects to their indigenous roots as well as to the best in their Christian roots, especially to their traditions of working for social, economic, and ecological justice.

I have also learned that only a modest number of African Americans are familiar with the story of Luther. After all, like Latinos, they are not of European descent or part of European culture. One link they have lies in the name of their own hero and protester, Dr. Martin Luther King, Junior. Of course, Martin Luther committed ecclesial disobedience five hundred years before Gandhi and King committed civil disobedience. And while Gandhi and King were smarter and more purposeful in keeping their disobedience non-violent, Luther unleashed the pent-up anger of the peasants, which sadly resulted in tens of thousands of deaths.

Thus, thanks to Gandhi and King, much progress has been made in steering social outrage into more positive directions than in Martin Luther's day. Dr. Howard Thurman, grandson of a slave, well-known preacher, and founder of the Church for the Fellowship of All Peoples in San Francisco is one of the voices in this effort. He writes about how dominant Christianity "betrayed Jesus" and develops this theme in his book *Jesus and the Disinherited*, a volume so important to King that he took it with him all thirty-nine times he was sent to jail. In his day, Martin Luther saw a similar reality to that of Howard Thurman. Thus there is a deep link between the two movements and forces of social change: the Protestant revolt of the sixteenth century and the civil rights movement of the twentieth century. King and Luther are connected by more than name.

I can only hope that people—including parish members—will study, discuss, and debate this book and will be inspired to act. After all, a thesis is something to be debated, and ninety-five of them provide a great deal of fuel for debate. Perhaps we need a New Reformation Sunday—maybe a New Pentecost Sunday—during which these ninety-five theses could be nailed to wooden frames outside all our cathedrals and churches in order to sound the alarm and get the spirit moving once again.

Suggested Bibliography

Anderson, Marvin Lee. On Hearing the 'Inner Word of God': The Appeal to the Common People in Reformation Germany. Toronto: University of St. Michael's College doctoral thesis, 2005.

Anderson, Walter Truett. Reality Isn't What It Used To Be. New York: HarperCollins, 1990.

Berry, Jason, and Gerald Renner. Vows of Silence: The Abuse of Power in the Papacy of John Paul II. New York: Free Press, 2004.

Berry, Thomas, and Brian Swimme. The Universe Story. San Francisco: Harper SanFrancisco, 1992.

Boff, Leonardo. Church: Charism and Power: Liberation Theology and the Institutional Church. New York: Crossroad, 1985.

Bonhoeffer, Dietrich. Letters and Papers from Prison. New York: Touchstone Press, 1997.

Boswell, John. Christianity, Social Tolerance, and Homosexuality. Chicago: University of Chicago Press, 1980.

Chenu, M. D. Nature, Man and Society in the Twelfth Century. Chicago: University of Chicago Press, 1968.

Chilton, Bruce. Rabbi Jesus. New York: Doubleday, 2000.

Chodrin, Pema. When Things Fall Apart. Boston: Shambhala, 1996.

Crossan, John Dominic, and Jonathan L. Reed. In Search of Paul. San Francisco: Harper SanFrancisco, 2004.

Fiorenza, Elisabeth Schussler. In Memory of Her: A Feminist Theological Reconstruction of Christian Origins. New York: Crossroad, 1984.

———. *Invitation to the Book of Revelation*. Garden City, N.Y.: Image Books, 1981.

Fox, Matthew. *Creativity: Where the Divine and the Human Meet*. New York: Jeremy Tarcher, 2004.

———. *One River, Many Wells: Wisdom Springing from Global Faiths*. New York: Jeremy Tarcher, 2000.

———. *Original Blessing*. New York: Jeremy Tarcher, 1983.

———. *Sins of the Spirit, Blessings of the Flesh: Lessons for Transforming Evil in Soul and Society*. New York: Harmony Books, 1999.

———. *The Coming of the Cosmic Christ*. San Francisco: Harper and Row, 1988.

Garrison, Jim. *America as Empire: Global Leader or Rogue Power?* San Francisco: Berrett-Koehler, 2004.

Harvey, Andrew. *The Direct Path*. New York: Broadway Books, 2000.

Jencks, Charles, ed. *The Post-Modern Reader*. New York: St. Martin's Press, 1992.

Korten, David. *When Corporations Rule the World*. West Harford, Conn.: Kumarian Press, 1995.

Lakoff, George. *Don't Think of an Elephant! Know Your Values and Frame the Debate*. White River Junction, Vt.: Chelsea Green Publishing, 2004.

Luther. DVD and VHS. Directed by Eric Till. Los Angeles, Calif.: MGM, 2004.

Macy, Joanna. *World as Lover, World as Self*. Berkeley: Parallax Press, 1991.

Macy, Joanna, with John Seed, Pat Fleming, and Arne Naess. *Thinking Like A Mountain: Towards a Council of All Beings*. Stony Creek, Conn.: New Society, 1988.

Nestingen, James A. *Martin Luther: A Life*. Minneapolis: Augburg Press, 2003.

Sheldrake, Rupert, and Matthew Fox. *Natural Grace*. New York: Doubleday, 1977.

Soelle, Dorothee. *Beyond Mere Obedience*. New York: Pilgrim Press, 1982.

Thich Nhat Hanh. *Living Buddha, Living Christ*. New York: Riverhead Books, 1995.

Thurman, Howard. *Jesus and the Disinherited*. Richmond, Ind.: n.p., 1981.

Wills, Garry. *Papal Sin: Structures of Deceit*. New York: Doubleday, 2000.

Resources

The following materials are produced by the Friends of Creation Spirituality. For information on acquiring these and any other available CDs, DVDs, or cassettes, please visit www.matthewfox.org

A Christianity for the 21st Century (two-DVD set). A lecture by Matthew Fox followed by a question-and-answer dialogue.

Beyond Empire: The Next Step to Spiritual Maturity (CD). A dialogue on economics and spirituality with Matthew Fox and David Korten.

One River, Many Wells (DVD). A lecture by Matthew Fox based on his book of the same title.

Connecting Chaos to Compassion (CD). Matthew Fox discusses what the wisdom traditions of the world teach us about movement through chaos to effective compassion.

From Tribalism to Community (DVD). Presentations by both Matthew Fox and Frances Moore Lappe at the EarthSpirit Rising 2005 conference on ecology, spirituality, and community.

Radical Prayer (Cassette and CD). A curriculum on using the power of prayer to change our world, this 6-session course covers: what prayer is and why it works; recovering the Sacred Masculine and Sacred Feminine; exploring the "dark night of the soul"; deep ecumenism, lessons from history's great mystics in every tradition; and more.

Hildegard von Bingen in Portrait (DVD). The visionary Hildegard (1098–1179) produced major works of theology and music and used the curative powers of music and natural objects for healing. Produced by the BBC, this four-hour DVD includes a complete rendition of her opera, a movie of her life, her paintings, and interviews with Matthew Fox and other scholars.

Contact Information

For information on the Cosmic Mass, including specifics on opportunities for learning how to create and produce the Cosmic Mass in your community, please visit www.thecosmicmass.org.

For information about hosting lectures or workshops by Matthew Fox, please contact Dennis Edwards at 33dennis@sbcglobal.net.

To join discussions on *A New Reformation*, please visit www.matthewfox.org.

About the Author

Matthew Fox was a member of the Dominican Order for thirty-four years and is the author of twenty-six books. He holds a doctorate in spiritual theology from the Institut Catholique de Paris.

In the 1970s Fox developed the theology of Creation Spirituality as a way to integrate the wisdom of Western spirituality and global indigenous cultures with the emerging scientific understanding of the universe and the creativity of art. Creation Spirituality has its roots in the earliest formulations of the Judeo-Christian wisdom tradition celebrated especially by mystics of medieval Europe. Creation Spirituality provides a holistic perspective from which to address the critical issues of our times, including the honoring of the feminine, the celebration of hope, the promotion of social and ecological justice, and the promotion of interfaith understanding. In pursuing these goals, Creation Spirituality has sought to revitalize education, ritual, work, and spirituality in the spirit of what Fox calls deep ecumenism.

Seeking to establish a pedagogy that was friendly to learning spirituality, in 1977 he formed an Institute in Culture and Creation Spirituality, which ran for seven years at Mundelein College in Chicago and twelve years at Holy Names College in Oakland, California.

Cardinal Ratzinger, head of the Roman Catholic Church's Congregation for the Doctrine of the Faith, silenced him for one year (from 1989 to 1990) and three years later expelled him from the Order and terminated the program at Holy Names College.

The principle objections to Fox's work on the part of the Catholic Church's Congregation for the Doctrine of the Faith were that he is a "feminist theologian," that he calls God "Mother" (Fox has proved the medieval mystical tradition did the same), that he prefers "Original Blessing" to "Original Sin," that he calls God "child," that he associates too closely with Native Americans, and that he does not condemn homosexuals.

Rather than disband his unique and ecumenical faculty, Fox started the University of Creation Spirituality, now Wisdom University, in 1996 in Oakland. Fox continues his connection there as president emeritus and as a teaching professor.

His effort to reawaken the West to its own mystical tradition has included reviving awareness of Hildegard of Bingen, Meister Eckhart, and the mysticism of Thomas Aquinas, as well as interacting with contemporary scientists who are also mystics.

Fox's books have received numerous awards. His titles include:

The Coming of the Cosmic Christ: The Healing of Mother Earth and the Coming of a Global Renaissance

Confessions: The Making of a Post-Denominational Priest

Creation Spirituality: Liberating Gifts for the Peoples of the Earth

Hildegard of Bingen's Book of Divine Works with Letters and Songs (editor)

Illuminations of Hildegard of Bingen

In the Beginning There Was Joy

Manifesto for a Global Civilization (with Brian Swimme)

Meditations with Meister Eckhart

Natural Grace: Dialogues on Creation, Darkness, and the Soul in Spirituality and Science (with Rupert Sheldrake)

One River, Many Wells: Wisdom Springing from Global Faiths

Original Blessing: A Primer in Creation Spirituality

Passion for Creation: The Earth-Honoring Spirituality of Meister Eckhart

Prayer: A Radical Response to Life

The Physics of Angels: Exploring the Realm Where Science and Spirit Meet (with Rupert Sheldrake)

The Reinvention of Work: A New Vision of Livelihood for Our Time

Religion USA: Religion and Culture by way of Time Magazine

Sheer Joy: Conversations with Thomas Aquinas on Creation Spirituality

Sins of the Spirit, Blessings of the Flesh: Lessons for Transforming Evil in Soul and Society

A Spirituality Named Compassion: Uniting Mystical Awareness with Social Justice

Western Spirituality: Historical Roots, Ecumenical Routes (editor)

Whee! We, wee All the Way Home: A Guide to a Sensual, Prophetic Spirituality

Wrestling with the Prophets: Essays on Creation Spirituality and Everyday Life

Fox has received the Peace Abbey Courage of Conscience Award, other recipients of which have included the Dalai Lama, Mother Theresa, and Rosa Parks. He has led a renewal of liturgical forms with the "Cosmic Mass," which mixes dance, live music including rap and techno, deejays, veejays, and contemporary art forms with the Western liturgical tradition.

He resides in Oakland, California.